Praise for *Irreplaceable*

"With reckoning at our doorstep, Kevin Kelley delivers an unmatched survival guide. Municipalities and real estate professionals, take heed: Kevin's tactical blueprint for creating soulful places is both revolutionary and essential. This isn't just another book—it's the lifeline you seek."

—Jeff Davenport, Cofounder & CEO, Tennyson, and
former SVP, Real Estate Research, Regions Bank

"*Irreplaceable* explores the profound impact of built environments on our sense of belonging and identity. Through engaging examples, Kevin Kelley illustrates how design choices shape our behaviors, emotions, and interactions with spaces. This thought-provoking book is a must-read for retail, brand marketing, real estate planning professionals, and general enthusiasts."

—Walt Zola, Chief Customer Officer, Newman's Own, Inc.

"Kevin Kelley has created a must-have playbook for any physical enterprise striving to stay relevant in an increasingly virtual world. A keen observer of how people convene, he shares vivid examples of creating trailblazing spaces that successfully bring people together at the intersection of commerce and community. His passion to 'make the everyday places of our lives extraordinary' speaks to all who believe the need for vibrant in-person engagement is more important than ever."

—John Bagan, President & CEO, Gelson's Markets

"*Irreplaceable* is a profound observation of our everyday spaces and places—built and natural—and the ways in which we humans navigate them in search of connection and meaning."

—Greg Fuson, Designer of Conferences, Experiences and
Engagement, PCBC (Pacific Coast Builders Conference)

"In this time of accelerated and unprecedented digital commerce, Kevin Kelley captures the necessity of *place* for all of humanity and provides a guide to those who want to create 'THE PLACE' in their respective operating segment! A must-read for all retail leaders."

—Tony Harris, former President/COO, Thornton's Inc.

"Kevin lays bare the importance of truly understanding people—beyond a 'consumer' or 'shopper' label—for anyone who touches the world of retail. As this world continues to evolve, *Irreplaceable* provides a framework and call to action for retailers to consider how their physical stores can themselves become a strategic asset and differentiator for the future."

—Jean Ryan, Vice President, Strategic Advisory, Daymon

"Kevin is able to visualize space unlike anyone I have met. He observes customers and their behavior like it is a sporting event. He's a master at strategy and branding and can smoothly transition his work into a concept. Best of all, he can articulate his thoughts with clarity, and using his highly descriptive language, our teams are able to implement them with meaning."

—Doug Lovsin, President, Freson Bros.

"Kevin uniquely understands human behavior and how structure, color, form, lighting, and graphics affect actions. I have truly enjoyed his and the team's insight and work over a thirty-year working relationship."

—Rich Niemann, Jr., President and CEO, Niemann Foods, Inc. (NFI)

"An extraordinary synthesis of science, design, psychology, and anthropology, *Irreplaceable* provides a rigorously insightful and pertinent work in the study of places and successful placemaking. At the forefront of his field as a practitioner, researcher, and thinker, Kelley makes enlightening connections in explaining the multifaceted aspects and interplay of people and space."

—Nick Zaharov, Vice President of Development, DWS Group (RREEF), and Faculty, Dollinger Master of Real Estate Development Program, University of Southern California

"In a world obsessed with digital landscapes, *Irreplaceable* brings us back to the irreplaceable value of physical space. Kevin takes us on a transformative journey through the places that make us human and offers a master class in the architecture of the soul. From the aisles of grocery stores to the showrooms of Harley dealerships, *Irreplaceable* offers a compelling vision for creating spaces that truly bring us together. A game-changer in the field of design and beyond."

– Andy Murray, Founder, Big Quest, and former SVP Marketing, Walmart

"I had the very good fortune of working closely with Kevin Kelley in reenergizing Charlotte's center city. A visit to Charlotte today will provide a look at Kevin's imprint in crowd-pleasing markets, attractive public spaces, popular restaurants, and a built-out light rail system. Through his vision, he showed that truly great cities are built through a collection of amenities, with a keen focus on character and creativity. A lesson I have carried with me."

—Rob Walsh, former NYC Small Business Services Commissioner during the Bloomberg Administration, and Adjunct Professor, Columbia University

"Everything that made for some of the most impactful and exciting projects in my career is all brought to life in this amazing new book from Kevin Kelley! If you want to accelerate sales and deliver extraordinary experiences for your shoppers, this is a must-read!"

—Craig Simon, Vice President, Customer Strategy, Mondelēz International & Cadbury

"I'm not surprised that I love Kevin Kelley's new book, *Irreplaceable*. His human behavior–centered design process is unlike anything I have seen or heard of from anyone else throughout my 43-year career working with architects. This is a book that anyone could enjoy and learn from."

—Mark C. Zweig, Entrepreneur-In-Residence, Sam M. Walton
College of Business, University of Arkansas; Chairman & Founder,
Zweig Group; and Author, *Confessions of an Entrepreneur*

"All great brands seek to develop a relationship, a dialogue, with their consumers beyond the simple transaction. Regrettably, for food manufacturers, the grocery store 'place,' where that engagement most directly exists, is built for shopping and operational efficiency, not the nurturing of that relationship. Kevin and Shook Kelley recognize that by creating a store, aisle, or section that enables the deepening of that relationship through environmental design cues, the shopper is more likely to engage with the brand. By creating a space that connects the positive thoughts and feelings they hold about the eating occasion with the product itself, the glorious moment of placing the brand in the basket is achieved."

—Ric Noreen, former Kraft Foods VP, Global Sales Strategy, and
Managing Partner, Waypoint Strategic Solutions, LLC

"The spaces Kevin and his team create, and his passion for activating our primal desire to go out and experience the world . . . all brought together for us to enjoy in *Irreplaceable*."

—Doug Scholz, SVP, Chief Operating Officer, California Grocers Association

"Kevin Kelley redefined branding for me in such a profound way that as the Chief Marketing Officer for Pepperdine, a top 100 nationally ranked university, I often asked myself when making critical decisions, 'What would Kevin do?' I'm so glad the world will get a sneak peek into the inner workings of Kevin's mind and the importance of creating meaningful experiences and sacred spaces that strengthen both brands and our communities in this revolutionary book."

—Rick Gibson, Senior Vice Chancellor, Pepperdine University

"More than a reflection on the past, *Irreplaceable* is a powerful call to action for the present and future. It urges us to cherish, preserve, and invest in these shared spaces as the lifeblood of our communities. As we increasingly feel disconnected, this book champions the importance of face-to-face interactions in fostering human connection. Most importantly, Kevin Kelley's book tells us how to build, maintain, and promote these places."

—Harvey Lung, Partner, Lung Rose Voss & Wagnild

"A fascinating deep-dive into human behavior and an in-depth guide to design spaces and places that bring us together, *Irreplaceable* is not only an inspiring and actionable read but much needed in our disconnected world to build cultures of belonging.

—Kim Dabbs, Global Vice President, ESG & Social
Innovation, Steelcase, and Author, *You Belong Here*

"Reading this book has been so refreshing and I love the stories that are told. Kevin Kelley reminds us why place matters and makes it clear that bringing people together is more important than ever. As our communities continue to fragment and subdivide into smaller and smaller digital pockets, that sense of place can become less and less obvious. There is a reason we go to conventions, sit in pubs, or visit the Harley dealership, and Kevin Kelley does a wonderful job of reminding us that, at the root of it all, being together is what it is to be human, and therefore, the importance of being proactive in creating extraordinary spaces is mission critical in today's world."
— Ross Binnie, Chief Brand Officer, The Cleveland Orchestra

"Kevin showed us that there is more to design than brick and mortar and how to develop the brand beyond our Harley-Davidson dealerships. With a tremendous depth of understanding of consumer psychology and physical spaces, Shook Kelley identified who we were at the core and helped us bring our brand to life via dealership locations, culture, and community, and frankly, it became the backbone of our team. Kevin and his team have the ability to turn an idea into a space (physical or virtual) where people gather and engage in unforgettable experiences."
—Scott Fischer, CEO, Scott Fischer Enterprises, and Owner, Thunderbird Harley-Davidson, Albuquerque, New Mexico, and Santa Fe Harley-Davidson, New Mexico

"In his new book, *Irreplaceable*, Kevin Kelley establishes the socioeconomic value of creating places for communities to convene and shares his authentic self: an avid student of human behavior. Through his gift for storytelling, Kevin explores the complex motivations and relationships that drive people to convene and demonstrates how architecture is about far more than a physical structure or design concept."
—Julie Kim, Vice President, Production, New York Philharmonic

IRRE PLACE ABLE

IRRE PLACE ABLE

How to Create
Extraordinary
Places That Bring
People Together

Kevin Ervin Kelley

Matt Holt Books
An Imprint of BenBella Books, Inc.
Dallas, TX

Matt Holt is an imprint of BenBella Books, Inc.
10440 N. Central Expressway
Suite 800
Dallas, TX 75231
benbellabooks.com
Send feedback to feedback@benbellabooks.com

BenBella and *Matt Holt* are federally registered trademarks.

Printed in the United States of America
10 9 8 7 6 5 4 3 2 1

Library of Congress Control Number: 2023034748
ISBN 9781637744741 (hardcover)
ISBN 9781637744758 (electronic)

Editing by Katie Dickman
Copyediting by Michael Fedison
Proofreading by Jenny Bridges and Sarah Vostok
Indexing by Beverlee Day
Text design and composition by PerfecType, Nashville, TN
Cover design by Sabrina Fan, Shook Kelley
Printed by Lake Book Manufacturing

"*To be at all—to exist in any way—is to be somewhere, and to be somewhere is to be in some kind of place . . . We live in places, relate to others in them, die in them. Nothing we do is unplaced . . . How could we fail to recognize this primal fact?*"

—Edward Casey

To my brother, Bryan, who taught me the value of making whatever environment you're in the best place to be.

CON TENTS

irreplaceable

[ir·re·place·able] *adjective*

Something so special it can't be replaced if lost or destroyed.

INTRO DUC TION

Ernie the Tow Truck Driver
Meets Kevin the Watcher

"YOU FOLLOWING ME?" I ASKED Ernie with a sly grin, trying to beat him to the punch before he blew my cover.

"Nah," Ernie replied, surprised to see me again. "I visit a few different dealerships each week."

"Why's that?" I asked.

"I like hanging out at Harley stores, but I can't always afford to buy something and I don't want them to throw me out for loitering," he said with a big smile, "so I move around stores."

Ernie's desire to "hang out" in the store told me a lot about his needs and wants and how we ought to be rethinking the purpose of the dealership, less as stores and more as clubhouses for wandering souls. It also gave me some insights on how we could better design them to ensure Ernie felt welcome to drop by anytime he wanted, regardless of whether he was buying something or just looking for something to do. Interestingly, nobody at the dealership ever told Ernie he couldn't hang out, but something about the environment communicated, "If you aren't buying anything, move along." And we needed to fix that perception.

I'd met Ernie, a tow truck driver by trade, the day before at another Harley dealership in a different town an hour away. He was sitting on a jet-black Harley with his arms stretched out to reach the chopper-like handlebars as his legs wrapped around a flaming red gas tank. I didn't know Ernie, and he didn't know me. But we were both participating in the standard ritual that plays out every day at Harley dealerships, where customers circle the store's interior and watch other customers sitting on bikes. This behavior of watching people "try on" products would seem creepy in a Zara or Banana Republic store, but it's perfectly normal at Harley dealerships.

So as Ernie did his part of the ritual, sitting on the bike, gripping the clutch, and balancing the massive machine under his feet, I did my part standing a few feet away with my arms folded, watching him test out the bike fit.

After a long pause, Ernie looked up and asked, "What do you think? Should I get it?"

"Sure!" I said. "It's a badass-looking bike!"

"I'm definitely thinking about it," he replied, "but it comes with a badass price tag too."

As Ernie and I got to talking, I learned he already owned two Harleys. I figured he must've been a lifelong rider and daredevil of sorts with thousands of miles under his "Born to Be Wild" belt. But when I asked where he likes to ride, he described his fear of taking his bike out on the highways and busy roads. As a result, he spends most of his bike time cruising up and down his cul-de-sac street, terrorizing his neighbors with his loud, thumping potato-sounding mufflers, which gave us both a laugh.

When I asked Ernie how he fell so hard for Harleys, he had these insightful words to say about his particular life stage: "My wife and I are in our midfifties, but she's got herself a bunch of hobbies and girlfriends to hang out with during the week. She's figured her life out," he said with a tinge of jealousy. "But now that the kids are all grown up and have lives of their own, what the hell am I supposed to do with my free time? I can only work so much, and golf and tennis aren't for me." He patted his belly. "If I didn't find something healthy to get into, I might end up hanging out at the pub, drinking myself silly, or worse, surfing the internet all day, which is a dangerous way to spend the rest of my life. I needed someplace to go outside work and home to hang out; so, on my days off, you can usually find me at one of the several different Harley stores in the area."

As Ernie and I talked more, he explained there aren't a lot of places he feels comfortable. "Blue Bottle Coffee, the Apple Store, and SoulCycle aren't my scene," he said. "You need six-pack abs and graphic design skills to hang out in those places. But when I visit a Harley store, I feel like the coolest guy in the room. This place makes me feel like a hero."

Although Ernie put himself out there more than most riders, his story wasn't all that different from many other customers (mostly men) I'd interviewed at thirty Harley dealerships across the U.S. Listening to their heartfelt stories about how much Harley means to them made me realize the problem they were trying to solve at the dealerships wasn't about transportation, recreation, or even status. The purchase they sought to acquire was "the end of loneliness for," as Ernie and I joked, "midlife-crisis-males-fading-in-strength."

While Ernie and others could easily buy an imported bike super cheap, those bikes didn't come with thousands of die-hard friends around the world that would give the shirt off their back if you were ever in a jam. And I couldn't help but calculate how much comfort that fellowship and bond must've been worth.

But it's not just the Ernies of the world who want to find an end to loneliness, a sense of belonging, and a place to call their own. So many of the audiences I interview in my line of work feel more isolated, dislocated, and displaced in this modern age of digital replacements. As Scott Galloway, a clinical professor of marketing at NYU Stern School of Business, said in a May 2023 interview with the *Wall Street Journal*, "Most of the technologies we're coming up with, or a lot of them, are pouring fuel on this flame of loneliness, where we're finding reasonable facsimiles of a relationship. Social creates this illusion that you have a lot of friends, but you don't experience friendship."

I've spent my life trying to bring people together through the timeless interactions and primal qualities of place. Being an architect, for me, isn't about creating beautiful *objects* for the wealthy or designing twisted, geometric design pretzels for the cultural elite; it's about making people from all walks of life feel beautiful, valued, and important in a world that doesn't always see them that way. But I *see* these folks every day because my job is to make the everyday places of our lives extraordinary.

THE MEANING OF CONVENING

When people learn I'm an architect, I can see the excitement in their eyes as they relay something they read about Frank Lloyd Wright or saw regarding Frank Gehry or the late Zaha Hadid. And the next question they inevitably ask me is: "What kind of projects do you design?" They hope I'll say mega-tall skyscrapers, modern museums, or vacation homes in Aspen. But when I tell them I mostly design grocery stores, convenience stores, pet stores, gyms, restaurants, bars, and the like, I can see their initial letdown before their eventual curiosity rises about how these places function and they share their personal opinions about what's wrong with them. Suffice it to say: I get a lot of suggestions.

Standing around for weeks on end watching people look at Harleys may not be for everyone, and it created an awkward moment when I first met my wife and told her how I spend my days in disguise as a customer. But it's what I do. I'm the guy who pulls up a lawn chair in a parking lot to watch people walk in and out of a steak buffet chain, and I'm the guy who studies consumers buying Fig Newtons in the cookie and cracker aisle of a grocery store. It's an odd job. My passion, though, is watching people go about their typical days in coffee shops, retail stores, or institutional facilities and noticing when they feel pleased or frustrated by their environments. But I'm not just a watcher. I'm also a fixer, adjuster, tinkerer, rethinker, and experience designer.

This fixation with watching people and tinkering with the atmospherics of everyday environments has been with me for as long as I can remember. As a kid, I was unusually observant. I could tell by the way someone walked into a room, where they stood, and how they sat whether they felt comfortable with their surroundings. I'd study lines at the post office, workers eating lunch in break rooms, and customers picking up prescriptions at the drugstore. I couldn't help but imagine how to make those situations more enjoyable before going home to draw design solutions at the kitchen table.

Despite my parents' questioning this eccentric behavior, I used our family home as a daily test lab. I was constantly turning light levels down, music dials up, and rearranging furniture to see how it impacted my family's mood and quality of interactions. And when I got bored with our family room, I'd move on to my teachers' classrooms and friends' bedrooms. But eventually, I had to find a bigger playing field to feed my appetite for improving the quality of places. Hence, I became an architect.

In 1992, I cofounded a strategic design firm with my good friend and lifelong mentor, Terry Shook. While the two of us came from different places and were at different career stages, I'd never met anyone who cared as much about developing healthy, vibrant, and inclusive communities—whether in retail, housing, education, or cities—as Terry. As a new firm, our first order of business was to persuade two talented designers we'd worked with in prior organizations, Frank Quattrocchi and Stan Rostas, to join our enterprise, both of whom became founding partners. Although we were all educated as architects, the tie that bound us together was a deep-seated belief that great things happen at the intersection of commerce and community. Armed with nothing more than our passionate vision, we set out to create a new multidisciplinary field called *convening*, which we define as the art and science of bringing people together around an idea, forum, and experience. This process integrates the best ideas, principles, and thinking from business, science, and design into a "clinic" approach where you have many experts from different fields (architecture, interior design, urban planning, branding, advertising, marketing, cultural anthropology, graphic design, merchandising design, etc.) analyzing the same problem and coming up with different ways to solve it.

Since we were a small firm initially, every project was a group effort. But it didn't take long for us to figure out Terry was good with acres and me inches. Terry had a remarkable talent for large-scale planning projects, whereas I focused more on intimate-scaled environments. My first love and taste of success was in restaurant and bar design. Frank and I created many successful and award-winning restaurant concepts together. Terry, however, asked me to help out on an assignment with a client he had a prior relationship with, the Southeast grocery store chain Harris Teeter. As Terry and Stan led the herculean effort to design a radical new prototype store concept across multiple states that ultimately won numerous awards, including Retail Store of the Year in 1997, I took on the job of developing a less sexy renovation program for upgrading their existing stores. I wasn't excited about working on a grocery store, but much to my surprise, a new love affair with this practical side of the food world was born. Like meeting your future spouse through a best friend, I'm forever grateful to Terry for making that initial introduction.

Today, thirty years later, I'm considered an expert in all things food-related, ranging from grocery and convenience stores to restaurants, cafés, bars, and food halls. While I've worked for scores of food-related brands such as Whole Foods, Kroger, Fry's, Kraft, Nabisco, Cadbury, and Smucker's among hundreds of regional companies and mom-and-pop shops, I've also worked with countless non-related food brands and entities, such as urban districts, universities, professional sports teams, and performing art institutions like the Cleveland Orchestra. In between, I've taught design, branding, and marketing courses at my alma mater, UNC Charlotte, and Harvard University, alongside my hero Gene Kohn, one of the most prolific designers of skyscrapers in the world and the founder of KPF, who sadly passed away at the age of ninety-two while I was writing this book.

BEING OBSESSIVE ABOUT HUMAN BEHAVIOR IS GOOD FOR BUSINESS AND HUMANITY

When we started our firm, the principles, tools, and techniques we developed were just theories on how business, social science, and design could intertwine to make a more effective process for building places that bring people together. But with over thirty years of experience, we now have a comprehensive library of case studies proving how environment affects behavior in a variety of commercial and institutional settings.

On average, my team and I increase foot traffic by 25 percent and sales by 18 to 86 percent without changing the product, prices, quality, or service levels—just the environment. But it's not only the sales lift clients seek. Sometimes they want to increase the frequency of visits, average dwell times in an aisle, and product experimentation. And other times, they want to change the overall perception and meaning of their brand to be more relevant to the times, yet distinct from competitors.

Most architects think in terms of feet and yards, but the strategic design assignments my clients ask my Los Angeles–based principals—Jennifer Kim, Sabrina Fan, and Jennifer Ochoa—to work on are down to inches of behavioral design and perception management. This level of detailed focus requires an in-depth knowledge of how the human body, mind, eyes, senses, and emotions work together subconsciously to influence decisions when navigating places.

For most of my career, my team and I have served as ghost designers for our clients' projects. We've never needed or wanted the credit for this work. Our goal is for our clients' projects to look like a natural extension and expression of them, much like a good speechwriter would for their candidate. But since the advent of the internet, the overwhelming infusion of Wall Street dollars into digital startups, and the profusion of corporate mergers and acquisitions, combined with the devastating impact the pandemic caused, we've been concerned about the survival of everyday places that make up our lives—local shops, grocery stores, cafés, office buildings, performing arts venues, live theater, and college campuses. These factors have contributed to accelerating a Replacement Economy where physical places have become endangered species, some of which are already at risk of going extinct. And I can't stand by and let that happen.

My concerns about saving places go beyond just the health of local businesses and the need for social engagement. I worry about our decreasing ability to focus and be present with loved ones as well as the cognitive development of children's brains.

We all arrive in this world somewhat unfinished, and venturing out into the sensory-rich environment is a critical part of our developmental process. As David Eagleman states in his 2020 book *Livewired: The Inside Story of the*

Ever-Changing Brain: "Nature's approach to growing a brain relies on receiving a vast set of experiences such as social interaction, conversation, play, exposure to the world and the rest of the landscape of normal human affairs. This strategy of interaction with the world allows the colossal machinery of the brain to take shape from a relatively small set of instructions."

If our youth played video games and surfed the internet all day, communicated with others only through text, Instagram, and TikTok, wrote their school reports through ChatGPT, and didn't have these "worldly" experiences much in the future, we'd be concerned. But they're already heading in this direction as the average daily screen time among teens (ages 13 to 18) is 8 hours and 39 minutes and growing. As terrifying as that sounds, adults aren't far behind as they spend 413 minutes (just under 7 hours) per day online, a few inches away from their screens. That's equivalent to 105 days a year! What if you could get back all the days you spent online over the last decade? What would you do with them? Put them back into more future online activities, such as social media? Or invest them in meeting with friends, playing with your kids in the backyard, or taking on that passion project you always wanted to pursue?

The repeated argument we hear from tech titans for why these technological devices and apps are lifesavers is that they save us time and money, remove friction, and can reach around the globe while making our lives easier. But shouldn't some things in life require effort? I believe there is a direct correlation between the effortfulness of human activity and the meaning and payoff it provides. Not all friction is bad, and not everything has to be uber-convenient or ruthlessly efficient. Yes, writing a handwritten love letter to your partner requires more effort than sending a text or using ChatGPT, but the personal effort makes it more meaningful. Meeting with your business associates in person versus on Zoom takes more time, energy, travel, and coordination, but it also facilitates stronger bonds and engenders more effective communication because words are just a small part of human connection. While we can connect with hundreds of thousands of "friends" at the touch of our keyboard and decide whether we "like" or want to "follow" them, something about this easier, frictionless approach doesn't feel like friendship, a community, or a viable replacement for in-person relationships.

This issue of *effort* versus *ease* affects almost every other aspect of our lives. For instance, ordering food from Postmates every night is much easier than cooking at home. And if their plans work out, it might even become cheaper. But there is something about handpicking our ingredients and making a meal with our loved ones that connects us more intimately to food, making the experience of eating more rewarding, healthy, and grounding. Similarly, getting rid of school campuses and taking all our courses at home online may be more efficient and scalable, but there is something equally instructional about the social experience of attending school with others that is just as educational, developmental, and essential for preparing students for the world as the class topics alone. Intelligence without social skills and the regular practice of interacting and cooperating with others makes for a dangerous society.

Historically, we haven't needed a guidebook for saving place, just as we haven't needed one about saving water or air until recently, because place has been with us as a naturally occurring part of our lives for thousands of years. But if water or air were going extinct, as many experts tell us they are, people would want to know more about how to save them. It's the same for public places. Many places that have been standard fixtures in our lives are hanging on by a thread. We can't just assume they'll save themselves without our intervention.

WHAT'S IN STORE FOR THIS BOOK

This book is for those who own, manage, design, or inhabit a physical place or human experience as part of their business model or operation. These places include anywhere people convene in the public realm, whether a local grocery store or pub, a religious facility or an office building, a bowling alley or university, or an urban district or zoo. This book is also for parents, teachers, and students wanting to know more about how the environment of a place affects human behavior, social interactions, and our mental health and well-being.

Broken into four parts, we begin Part I by digging into the timeless role public markets have played in society since the dawn of modern civilization. I'll propose a middle-path language that ensures those who fund places—and those who design them—put aside their competing agendas to find common ground and see eye to eye on what they need to do to make places work in this day and age of retail giants and tech disruptors. We'll establish a foundation for creating the types of experiences people can't help but want to gather around—something I call the "Bonfire Effect."

In Part II, we dive into how humans see, perceive, and interpret their environment. We'll look at the pivotal role the senses and emotions play in subconsciously attracting and engaging people in their surroundings. We'll examine why some places drain people's batteries, whereas others fill their tanks with energy and inspiration. And we'll peel back the curtain on why some situations and scenes make us laugh, cry, and shout out loud as part of the theater of life.

In Part III, "How to Build Your Own Bonfire," we lay out our innovation system chock-full of valuable tips, techniques, and frameworks to come up with game-changing ideas and manage the success of your place well into the future. While our firm works in a wide variety of industries, I'll use many examples from the strategic design work we do in the grocery store industry because these stores are common ground places almost everyone is familiar with, relies upon, and has strong opinions about. It might surprise you how much an office park, airport, or symphony hall can learn about consumer behavior from studying the design logic of a supermarket.

Finally, in Part IV, we'll explore how our tools and techniques can help those audiences who don't always have access to good design and are regularly overlooked by the professionals. We'll use examples of a blighted urban district with an initial annual operating budget of only $20,000 and an unfashionable restaurant chain to illustrate how our unique framework can recast a place's brand image in the market and put them on the path to success.

PLACE MATTERS

Most of us know something is "not right" with how people treat each other today. Our civil discourse and social divide is coarsening. We can feel the extreme polarization, the disparity between the rich and poor, and the dwindling economic opportunities for most people to get ahead, much less make ends meet. We sense something happening underfoot in the world of commerce, trade, and job opportunities where small shops on the main street struggle to survive, while big-data-intensive mega-corporations continue to expand, dominate, and infiltrate every intimate corner of our lives. And we can see the immense advantages the retail giants and tech titans have over small businesses and the incredible influence billionaires have on media, politicians, and public policy. In our not-so-distant past, we met at the local pub, diner, or town hall to discuss and debate issues and demand change when needed. But today, it's hard to find that neighborhood pub, much less a town square where engaged citizens can bump elbows and discuss the future of our society. So we air our complaints anonymously online, which is about as effective as putting a message in a bottle and throwing it in the Atlantic Ocean, hoping the right person on a distant shore will read it and care enough to do something with it.

Deep down inside us is this troubling sense that human connection, engagement, and civility are dissolving right before our eyes, but we aren't entirely sure what to do about it. Even though that assessment may sound bleak, where else does human connection happen? X (formerly Twitter)? Zoom? Instagram? While place doesn't solve all these problems, it's an essential first step in bringing us back together as friends, neighbors, and strangers to meet and connect in person instead of picking each other apart in faceless online forums and chat rooms. "It may be, in the end," James Surowiecki reminds us in his illuminating book, *The Wisdom of Crowds*, "that a good society is defined more by how people treat strangers than by how they treat those they know."

As a lifelong advocate and champion for social engagement in the public realm, I'll argue that the loss of place plays a significant role in this anxiety and unease. But you won't hear me propose handouts for those who run places. Nor do I expect the government to subsidize physical places out of pity or some sense of nostalgia. Instead, I want businesses and institutions that have a place as a critical part of their operation to learn how to compete better and win people over to their side by playing a different game and running a different race that taps into the timeless power of the human experience.

While the Amazons of the world may have a lock on price, variety, and convenience, they don't have a monopoly on joy, delight, surprise, and social bliss. There's a massive opportunity for those who design places, whom I call "place-makers," and those who fund and run places, whom I call "place-operators," to adopt a new frame of mind and equip themselves with the right set of tools for making the crucial places of our society *irreplaceable*.

PART ONE

The Bonfire Effect: What Would You Crawl Through Mud to Acquire?

"Serendipitous connections become less likely as increased communication narrows our tastes and interests. Knowing and caring more and more about less and less. This tendency may increase productivity in a narrow sense while decreasing social cohesion."
—Robert Putnam, *Bowling Alone*

WHEN MOST PEOPLE HEAR THE words "South Florida," their minds go straight to vacation mode—either that or Pitbull, Don Johnson, or Scarface, depending on their era. I grew up, however, on the "other" side of the Sunshine State: the swamplands off Okeechobee Road.

To get to my neck of the woods, you'd have to endure a bumpy ride that could rattle the fillings right out of your teeth. At the end of that dirt road, you'd then make a hard right turn into cypress tree swamps chock-full of gators, cottonmouth snakes, and a never-ending assault of bloodthirsty mosquitoes.

To pass the days in this rural community, many of us spent our free time building elaborate swamp buggies that could traverse any terrain like something out of a low-budget Mad Max movie. This quest may seem like an odd hobby. But the rationale for doing so was simple: we couldn't wait till Sunday rolled around so we could head out to the Mudflats.

The Mudflats were the "it" place to see and be seen in our community. The area encompassed a serene, water-filled oasis two miles out into the open, horizonless swamp. Somewhere in the middle of this vast, flat nothingness, a mound of sand rose out of the coffee-colored marsh like a redneck Riviera beach resort. It may not be most people's idea of paradise or postcard-worthy material, but the Mudflats were our sacred place of meaning. We'd sweat grease and drop driveshafts all week to get there and never regretted a second once we arrived. We drank anything liquid, ate paper plates full of exotic critters like catfish, gator, or cooter (turtle), and sang our hearts out to redneck anthems like "Free Bird." But the primary reason people were willing to risk life and limb to get to this middle-earth destination was because of what went up once the sun went down—something I call the "Bonfire Effect."

As part of our ritual, an hour before sunset, a self-organizing group of family, friends, and strangers would work together under the guidance of a self-appointed "bonfire master," collecting anything that burned. We then took these sticks, twigs, and empty beer cases and created an enormous pyramid-shaped bonfire before siphoning off some gas and striking a match.

We all did our part in an unusually cooperative manner, but it was the "bonfire master"—Chief Brand or Chief Experience Officer in today's LinkedIn world—who led the tribe and created our vibe. Not only did they have to ensure the fire didn't grow too big or shrink down too small, but they also had to help synchronize a group of strangers to feel connected to something larger than themselves. This harmonious quality of the "group experience" is what Swiss psychiatrist Carl Jung called "participation mystique." One of his close collaborators, Marie-Louise von Franz, described Jung's insight further as "a psychological condition in which various inanimate objects and people participate with each other in a mystical manner, [and] are connected with each other beneath the surface of consciousness." It's heady stuff, I know. But it speaks to the power of places to bring people together in ways that make them friendly, neighborly, and "in this together."

While I've had the privilege to travel the world and see many amazing places, when I reflect on the most meaningful moments of my life, those bonfire moments at the Mudflats rank high on the list. We came together. We toasted the good life. And we bonded around magical moments of community bliss.

FROM THE MUDFLATS TO MELROSE

As I sit in my L.A. office today, looking down into the hip, funky, and fashion-couture district of Melrose Avenue, I realize I couldn't be farther away from those monster mudder swamplands. Yet, I still see the power of the "Bonfire Effect" everywhere I go, from the daily crowds waiting in line to get one of the 2,500 hot dogs served every day at legendary Pink's Hot Dogs to the annual sixty-thousand-plus visitors who travel great distances to snap a photograph of themselves standing in front of the "pink wall" phenomenon at the Paul Smith store. And, lucky for me, I get to play a role in building these bonfire moments for major brands and institutions.

The core principle my team and I use in our strategic design work is an extension of Jung's idea, which we call "place-participation mystique." I define this quality of place as: "A situational experience where people feel emotionally connected to a place and its occupants because of a sense of shared values, purpose, and identity." This process aims to enhance the value of place by creating experiential rewards and a social payoff that can't be found elsewhere.

We all have bonfire moments. I'd bet you've got your own version of a sacred place that holds special meaning, a magical place you'd crawl through mud to get to. It could be an old punk-rock club or a funky neighborhood pizza parlor. Or perhaps a nostalgic Irish pub. It could have even been hanging out at your local mall, which iconic 1980s films like *Fast Times at Ridgemont High* captured perfectly for my generation.

Typically, these sacred places don't mean much to outsiders. But to insiders, that's part of their allure, as they contain vital meaning, a deep sense of belonging, and nostalgic memories worth fighting for and risking time, money, and effort to experience. I learned long ago that nothing gets people more vocal and communities more activated than the prospect of tearing down a personally sacred place—even something as mundane as an old bowling alley, diner, or a local bookstore where life-shaping memories originated.

Whether we're conscious of it or not, we can't escape being in a place. All of our activities and memories happen within a physical setting and environment. Similarly, all of our thoughts and ideas about things, people, and places occur somewhere, and this experience shapes our perception of them—for better or worse—in impressionable ways. Memory-making is still happening in places today. But perhaps with less reverence, meaning, and experiential quality than we saw in the past when glorious department stores, iconic post offices, and palatial movie theaters lined our main streets and commercial boulevards. Despite our incredible advances in health, transportation, computing, and science, the quality of everyday places today seems more brutal and less human. Homes feel bigger but cheaper. Streets feel wider but harsher. And buildings appear more modern but less friendly. So much of the built environment today is about quantity and efficiency, not the quality of human experience and community engagement. Most concerning, many places today don't facilitate connection to others, much less provide inviting public spaces for those activities to happen. On the rare occasions we do get some architectural buildings that aren't about efficiency, it's usually some over-the-top public spectacle or abstract art experiment, like an upside-down building, or the avant-garde Blobitecture style, such as the Museum of Pop Culture, which the *New York Times* architectural critic Herbert Muschamp described as "something that crawled out of the sea, rolled over, and died."

While we like to believe that humans shape and control our environment, we underestimate how much our environments shape and influence us. We like to say we're "in" an environment, but the environment is as much "in us" as the food we eat. Whether that daily diet consists of junk food, fast food, or healthy food, what we ingest affects our bodies, minds, energy levels, quality of life, and longevity more than we realize. Like our modern-day diet, many people live and work in unhealthy places that leave them starving for human connection, hungry for social interaction, and craving sensory stimulation. Similarly, many businesses and institutions operate in environments that stunt their growth, weaken their value proposition, and put them at significant risk of "going out of business" because they lack the vital nutrients and essential ingredients needed to survive in our current era of competitive alternatives and digital replacements.

As wild and exotic as the Mudflats may sound, there was something very primal, human, and healthy about a place that allowed a bunch of friends and strangers to come together, bond, and celebrate being in each other's presence. It's fair to say the place had a pull that compelled us to go through a lot of work, effort, and expense to "get there" and acquire that experience.

Many places I encounter today, however, don't possess this "pull" quality. Instead, they "push" their products and services on us through desperate deals, steals, and commodity appeals without fully considering there are much easier ways to get the same things online with less effort, friction, and hurdles.

My team and I are intimately aware of the plight everyday places face in trying to survive the tidal wave of tech disruptions and the onslaught of digital replacements. We don't believe that ultra-utilitarian buildings or public spectacle buildings will save most places in the future. Instead, with each client we work with, we ask ourselves:

- What would it take to get people to crawl through mud to experience this place?

- What kind of Bonfire Effect would we have to create to get strangers to put down their phones, make eye contact, and gather around a recreational focus to feel more connected to one another?

It's a tall order, but considering the aggressive incentives that online alternatives offer, this experience proposition of bringing people together can't be incidental or tangential. It must be a core part of the offering to make the trip worth the effort. So, instead of fixating on words like "speed," "convenience," "scale," "reach," and "cheap," we lean into the benefits and rewards of having a social and emotional experience in a society where an engaged life in the public realm seems to be evaporating.

The scarcity of the social experience is what actually creates the market.

And thinking about the market is an excellent place to discuss the first step in creating places and experiences people can't help but want to gather around.

The Great Value Exchange

"Exchange is 'one of the purest and most primitive forms of human socialization,' the sociologist Georg Simmel wrote in 1900; it creates 'a society, in place of a mere collection of individuals.' A market is a social construction."
—John McMillan, *Reinventing the Bazaar*

WHEN I TELL OTHER ARCHITECTS I work in retail, I often get a look of pity as if I sold out the virtues of architecture. Retail designers have always been considered second-class citizens in my profession because anything that includes cash registers, price tags, and neon signs is not "art," or so the reasoning goes.

During the early part of my career, I was also uncomfortable with architecture slumming around with the hucksters of retail. Like many creative types, I struggled to reconcile how cash registers and capitalism could fit into the purity of architecture as the idea of design and sales intermingling turned me off.

But no matter where I went in the "real world," I saw how commerce found its way into the built environment and enlivened buildings, streets, sidewalks, and cities with the pulse of human activity and social encounters. So, instead of running from retail, I confronted its impact on design head-on. After many years of intense interrogation and soul-searching, I began to see retail and commerce not as the enemy of architecture but as the social lubricant that makes places come alive with daily interactions, energy, and vitality. I witnessed how buying, selling, and trading brings people together, sparks random conversations, and fosters a greater sense of community and connection among strangers.

Despite my initial aversion to retail having any role in architecture, it was a statement by Fred Rogers of the TV show *Mister Rogers' Neighborhood* that inspired me to go all in: "I went into television because I hated it so, and I thought there was some way of using this fabulous instrument to be of nurture to those who would watch and listen."

Like Mr. Rogers's inability to "leave well enough alone," it was my frustration with how retail was being designed and developed in the 1980s—and my belief in its greater social purpose—that led my business partner, Terry Shook, and me to build a robust philosophy around convening people through the timeless concepts and rituals of the market.

THE MARKET IS A PART OF US

People often talk about retail as if it's something shallow, vain, and materialistic. But buying and selling goods is not as superficial as it might appear on the surface. Since the dawn of human civilization, people have been "going to the market." The ancient "agora" or "market" was the center of cities, not religious facilities, as many assume. On a basic level, people went to the market to trade tangible goods and services, but the idea of "exchange" goes much deeper than that.

First, the need for trade is primal. It's hardwired in humans to go "out there"—beyond the borders of their caves, villages, and living rooms—to find solutions to life's nagging problems. The person who made wheels from stones or the healer who cooked up cough syrup from tree bark was a lifesaver, and the local market provided a venue for that exchange of knowledge, wisdom, and advice to take place. Second, the market served as the town square and community center to share ideas, stories, cultures, traditions, news, politics, laughs, and smiles. Third, the market was where people learned about the "fashion of the times" in their community and found out "what's in" and "what's on its way out." Of equal or arguably more value, the market also provided people with a way to watch and observe others and learn social norms about how to behave in public while still expressing their unique social identities. Lastly, the market provided people with a desperately needed sense of escape from the confines of home and the drudgery of work. It gave them an outlet, occasion, and excuse to be somewhere else and somebody else other than a day laborer, mom or dad, or lonely bachelor or widow.

The market was—and still is to a large degree—the place to "see and be seen" in public by others. It's one of those essential "third places" outside of home and work, as Ray Oldenburg, the author of *The Great Good Place*, might describe it. The market provides a forum and medium for people to meet friends, family, and strangers in a safe, friendly, and prosocial setting.

We may not think about it much, but the face, clothes, shoes, and jewelry we wear at home and work usually differ from the ones we wear in public. Sure, we can now buy everything we need in our boxer shorts or pj's at home, but over time this isolation from other people can erode our sense of self and social identity. The presentation of self in the public market has many psychological, sociological, and anthropological benefits, as well as a sense of sensory theater, depending on the design and configuration of the place. Some places are more conducive for meeting and socializing with people than others. For example, a mixed-use outdoor shopping center does a much better job helping people interact, socialize, and foster community than, say, a utilitarian Kmart store does.

IS THE DIGITAL MARKET ALL WE NEED?

Many people assume the "market" has just moved online. They argue our "third places" are now happening on X, TikTok, and Instagram. To some degree, this presentation of self and cataloging of our social lives online is happening because of the incredible scale, reach, and convenience of digital advancements. Not to mention the exorbitant profits these digital entities generate by capturing our attention, harvesting our data, and selling our intimate details on the open market.

But something incredibly human and essential to society gets lost in translation in the digital expression of life. After all, we're social animals wired to be with and around other people in real life, not just from the chest up on a grainy 2D Zoom call. Nature designed us to see each other face-to-face. To make eye contact and sync up with others. To gauge their body language, catch their ever-so-slight facial inflections, and pick up on their tone of voice.

There is something dangerous and anti-human about a society of people— particularly kids—whose primary social interactions and relationships happen exclusively online. As social capital expert Robert Putnam says, "People divorced from community, occupation, and association are first and foremost among the supporters of extremism," and as citizens, we need to take that warning of disengagement from society seriously.

While "buying" something online may be cheap, convenient, and highly efficient, it's mostly a *transactional* activity. There's nothing emotional to connect with, belong to, or have a casual conversation with on a website. "Shopping" on the high street with your friends, however, or exploring the artisan delicacies offered at your local farmers market with your significant other, or even just having some idle chitchat with a salesperson is not only *relational* but experiential, social, and psychologically therapeutic for many. Incidental interactions like this stitch us together more than we realize.

These unique qualities and features of "shopping" need to be a pivotal part of the value equation place-makers offer as part of their place proposition. But far too many of them are fixated on imitating the strategies and techniques of the digital marketplace as opposed to leveraging the unique and proprietary benefits that make the human experience of place irreplaceable.

Hard as it may be for some businesses to accept today, places don't stand a chance of competing in the game of price, variety, or convenience anymore. They're much better off letting go of that contest and competing on the primal, timeless, and universal human dimensions of joy, delight, discovery, escape, community, and social bliss. The acquisition of material items is rooted in the core of humans, as Maslow's Hierarchy of Needs informs us. But once we get those basic needs met, we search for the deeper qualities and more evolved dimensions of life, such as belonging to a community, socializing with others, and experiencing the thrills of being alive, activating our senses, and strutting our stuff in public.

Only when people in a society get too much of one thing do they question how much they really want it in their lives. Initially, most of us welcomed technology into our homes with open arms and unfettered access. Technology was an exciting tool we could use to make our lives better. But instead of humans *using* technology as a tool, it now wants to *use* us as a tool to harvest and sell the data it reaps from us to the highest bidder, which has enormous market value.

The partnership between technology and Wall Street sees humans as a profit-making venture for investors to "make a killing" and become unicorn billionaires. Many of us, however, are now having second thoughts about all the "surveillance capitalism" operating in our lives. We're not as comfortable with Google tracking our every move, Facebook's outsized role in influencing politics, X's propensity to divide us into extreme camps, Instagram's effect on mental health and body-conscious concerns, and TikTok's ability to monetize our attention and shape our opinions, while potentially sharing our confidential conversations with foreign entities.

Recent college graduates, parents, business leaders, and politicians are increasingly asking themselves whether they want to live in a digital-only society with no local main street, shops, grocery stores, restaurants, gyms, or schools.

Based on countless consumer interviews across various industries my team and I have conducted, the short answer is people don't want to choose one over the other. Instead, they want a healthy balance of digital convenience, physical experience, social interaction, and community connection. Many of the same people we've spoken with are supporters of retailers incorporating a robust omnichannel approach that involves the best physical and digital benefits, or what some call "phygital." It's not a pretty word, but it speaks to the destination most retailers are heading toward by offering heightened

sensory in-store experiences while providing tremendous efficiency and convenience of digital tools. For physical venues to survive, they'll have to adjust
to selling different features, benefits, and qualities than before and learn how
to compete in a fierce, ruthless, and heavily-funded battlefield. But time is of
the essence, as the physical landscapes of our neighborhoods and communities are changing rapidly.

With over 353 million products available, Amazon alone accounts for 37.8
percent of the U.S. e-commerce market, making it the country's leading online
retailer. Every hour they are in operation, they take $17 million out of the mar-
ket. At the time of this writing, two of the largest grocery store chains, Kroger
and Albertsons, have agreed to merge in a $24.6 billion deal, which, according
to a *Guardian* article by Matt Krupnick in October 2022, "would give the
combined company control of nearly one-fifth of the U.S. grocery market, with
about 5,000 stores across 48 states." This same article quotes Stacy Mitchell,
a co–executive director of the Institute for Local Self-Reliance, a nonprofit
that helps communities attract grocery stores and other services, saying, "This
merger is incredibly dangerous. It's highly likely if it goes through, it will result
in more communities not having a grocery store."

Whether this particular merger gets approval or not, more consolidation
in general will happen in the retail and grocery industries, as smaller retailers
will have to merge or be acquired to compete against Amazon's monstrous
market size and buying power. But what will become of the local shops and the
neighborhood markets who don't want to merge or be part of a conglomerate?
They'll struggle to compete because they'll be excluded from the better pricing
terms the giants get. RF Buche, owner of Buche Foods and Gus Stops convenience stores, put it best in a January 2023 Bloomberg article: "We have no
leverage, no negotiation power whatsoever." According to the article, "When
R.F. Buche buys Cheerios to stock his grocery and convenience stores in rural
South Dakota, he pays $6.30 for an 18-ounce box. Walmart Inc. pays so much
less that it can sell the cereal to customers for just $4.78."

This disparity begs the question if this is what we genuinely want as a society: a handful of tech titans and retail giants controlling the food market and

dictating the vendor's terms and customer's prices, fewer local stores, and less daily human interaction.

We're much closer to that reality than we realize.

I'm all for technological advancement and retail competition. However, the current potential of a few tech titans and retail giants dominating the entire retail landscape and food supply chain makes me question our supposedly "free market economy" and whether it ultimately leads to better consumer options and market choices. If we don't establish some guardrails and protect these common ground places for people to meet in the universe as opposed to the metaverse, we're doomed to living lives of further isolation, dislocation, and alienation.

The best place to start this social facilitation is by maintaining the intersections of where commerce and community meet—whether that be a local pub, grocery store, or shopping center. But it requires the authors of places to come together and find common ground to better understand how to make their experience a core part of their proposition.

WHAT A DIFFERENCE WORDS CAN MAKE

While we take the complexity of building shopping centers, college campuses, skyscrapers, hotels, and performing arts facilities for granted, the number of eyes, hands, and agendas involved behind the scenes is massive and comparable to a military operation.

Building owners have to deploy platoons of managers, professionals, resources, and equipment to transform raw dirt or swampland into temples of consumption within incredibly tight schedules and budget parameters. The bankers, lawyers, accountants, regulatory agencies, and neighborhood review committees alone have the power to drive a perfectly sane person nuts, and that's not even counting the swarms of designers, engineers, planners, builders, suppliers, and vendors involved in shaping the final product. Needless to say, not all of these parties agree on the same process, much less the same definition of what victory looks like, and that's because they have different objectives and goals.

For the sake of our discussion, though, I'd like to simplify the parties into two admittedly broad categories:

1. **Clients**—which tend to be leaders steeped in business, management, finance, marketing, retail, and so on. Let's call them **Capitalists**.
2. **Designers**—which tend to be trained in the arts—not economics, business, or management—such as architects, interior designers, graphic designers, urban planners, and so on. Let's call them **Creators**.

Within any strategic endeavor, there is a built-in tension between these two parties. In simplistic terms, the Capitalists want to spend less money, reduce risk, and maximize their return on investment (ROI), while the Creators have a well-earned reputation to spend more and make less in an attempt to create art and build something aesthetically beautiful and poetically expressive.

This healthy tension makes for good art and business in the best scenarios. But in the worst cases, it can make for an internal war of competing agendas, which is more often the norm and is proving deadly to the viability of places in the current digital/generational/consolidation/replacement environment we live in today.

For example, terms like "marketing," "consumer behavior," "scalability," and "ROIs" don't sit well with Creators, their industry associations, and their past professors' dogmas. These business terms rub their academic hairs the wrong way and lack the integrity, purity, and primary aim of creating "art" as its central focus. Likewise, Capitalists aren't concerned about the abstract stylistic language of Parametricism, Deconstructivism, or Digital Morphogenesis or as obsessed about the visual interplay of geometries as architects are. The moment Capitalists bring up "sales per square foot," "foot traffic," and "revenue projections," the Creators feel like they're "selling out" and working for the big green machine instead of expressing their art.

On the Creator side, think "starchitects" like Frank Gehry, Bjarke Ingels, and the late Zaha Hadid, who determine a project's final shape. Or take the Spanish architect Santiago Calatrava, who has been known to roll up his drawings and go home when a client tries to compromise his "art" or reduce his budget, and he has so much design clout he usually gets his hostage terms met. And on the Capitalist side, think of real estate developers like Stephen M. Ross and the late Sheldon Adelson and Sam Zell as those who ultimately call the shots.

Despite Creators and Capitalists usually being civil, professional, and even accommodating to each other in meetings, I've regularly observed this dynamic of two essential parties having competing agendas, sometimes even hidden agendas, neutralizing or thwarting each other's objectives as they struggle to find common ground. (I once asked a legendary architect how his firm got such experimental, risky, and expensive architectural design concepts approved by his ultra-conservative, traditional clients. His answer: "I keep them in the 'floor plan' mode while the clock runs down, so there's no time for changes in the exterior elevation and facade treatments." Dishonest? Yes! But often applauded by the academy as "the artist knows best.")

So instead of trying to get Creators to embrace, much less understand, the complexities of Capitalists' goals, and Capitalists to fund the artistic follies and academic thesis statements of Creators, what's needed is a different language that can unite parties and combine the mutual goals and motivations of both audiences.

THE "GREAT VALUE EXCHANGE"

As obvious as it sounds, words exist to help us communicate with one another as efficiently and effectively as possible. But sometimes, words can have the opposite effect of turning off our ability to listen, much less understand the perspective of others. (Trigger words like "climate change," "deregulation," "gentrification," "liberal," and "conservative" can shut conversations down immediately.)

A classic example of this miscommunication in business is the word "branding." During the 1960s and '70s, the verb "branding" was more of an inside baseball term for advertising and marketing professionals. When most people outside of these professions heard the word "brand," they thought of Dove soap or Tide laundry detergent and not branding as a verb, process, or field of study. But the term "branding" is so common, pervasive, and ubiquitous today that people glaze over it, finding it outdated.

Yet branding—or the study of imbuing products and services with meaning and intangible qualities beyond the actual product—is timeless and offers tremendous value and insights for places. I learned early in my career that the use of the term "branding" made Creators cringe because they immediately think of selling, money, greed, snake oil sales tactics, and showmanship like that of P. T. Barnum. And when I use the term "branding" with many Capitalists, they think of logos, taglines, and promotional marketing material applied to a product like an aerosol spray instead of viewing it as a core part of the cultural meaning they should offer.

While I've had success getting Creators and Capitalists to agree on the importance of creating a Bonfire Effect in places, the harder challenge has been getting both audiences to see the critical intersection and interrelationship between commerce and community. To build a bridge between the Creators and Capitalists, I stopped using typical trigger words of "sales" and "art," and came up with the phrase the "Great Value Exchange" to capture our joint mission and target. Let's break the term down further:

- The word "Great" is very simple to get your head around. It points to the grand and historical origins of the market, which helps both Creators and Capitalists appreciate the timeless, universal qualities of famous places like the Grand Bazaar in Istanbul, Turkey, or Italy's oldest active mall, the Galleria Vittorio Emanuele II in Milan, or the Grand Bazaar of Isfahan that's stood since the early 1600s. Both sides usually agree that these historic places are sites of great architecture, great commerce, and great human interaction.

- The word "Value" is also simple. It points to providing people with something of importance or worth (whether tangible or intangible) that they're willing to leave their home or work to acquire. Again, it speaks to Creators and Capitalists as they both want to please the end user.

- Lastly, the word "Exchange" can be used as a noun in the name of a place or a physical structure. Or it can also be a verb as it describes a timeless human activity where both the buyer and the seller each have something of value—say fish for wheat or products for money—they'd like to exchange.

As I started using this term in the mid-1990s it became abundantly clear both sides of the aisle not only got the idea, but embraced it. The Creators like it because they see their work as an integral part of society that elicits positive emotions. They feel like they're creating a place of visual attraction—the market—that brings people together to enjoy their art. The Capitalists like it because it points to growth and dollar signs. They feel like they're carving out a unique position in the market of business. And I like it because it creates places where more meaningful human interactions can occur and where commerce and community can meet with a virtuous cycle.

If I wrote this book for Creators and bashed Capitalists for their lack of taste, they'd salute me. If this book was for Capitalists, and I slammed the Creators for not being grounded in reality, they'd applaud me. But this kind of thinking is an unnecessary and unproductive war of ideologies and beliefs that is destructive when retail and other place-based entities are being wiped out. Whether they realize it or not, both audiences need each other, and shopkeepers, restaurateurs, pub owners, and university presidents depend on them to build places that can survive and thrive in the new world we live in today.

Instead of measuring the success of a place by how much money it saves or how many design awards it achieves, the real test is how people react, behave, and frequent these places that are designed by Creators and produced by Capitalists.

Making the *audience* the star of place allows both Creators and Capitalists to get clear on what kind of payoff they need to provide to consumers in exchange for their time, energy, and expense. For that to happen, though, we need to clarify what we're offering the public: Is it a product or an experience? And what might change if the experience becomes the primary product of place?

CHAP TER TWO

The Work vs. Payoff Ratio of Place

"How many Americans having 'surfed' all the channels and, bored by it all, wouldn't like to slip on a jacket and walk down to the corner and have a cold one with the neighbors? Ah, but we've made sure there's nothing on the corner but another private residence . . . indeed, nothing at all within easy walking distance."

—Ray Oldenburg

SCAN THE NEWS ANY GIVEN week and you're bound to read at least one article proclaiming the death of the mall. They've been printing these obituaries, holding vigils, and planning funerals for these facilities since I began my career in a mall design firm in the late 1980s. Yet here we are thirty-five years later, still talking about their demise. That's not to say the mall's continuance is guaranteed, as there's been a thinning of the herd from 2,500 malls in the 1980s to less than seven hundred today. But it's remarkable the concept of the mall has held on this long.

When IPX—the world's largest provider of title insurance and real estate–related services—asked over a thousand Americans if they wished malls would make a comeback, 61 percent responded yes. The younger the shopper, the more avid their support for indoor shopping was. A whopping 66 percent of Gen Z and Gen X respondents were enthusiastic about malls maintaining a place in their lives, and 59 percent of millennials and 54 percent of baby boomers voted pro-mall too. So what's "dead" might be resurrected.

Though the "life and death of malls" makes for an entertaining debate, I'm more intrigued that people can't stop talking about them. It's not just investors, reporters, and analysts but everyday citizens who wade into the murky waters of this discussion to cast their opinions and place their bets on the mall's future. This level of engagement is because people still need, want, and yearn for some semblance of the ancient agora and the public marketplace in their lives, as described in the previous chapter. And while the mall might not be the ideal place to be today, nothing has come to fully take its place yet.

No matter if I'm working in a small town in Ohio or a mushrooming metropolis in the Philippines, I can always find a place the locals call "the mall." In some communities, these malls possess an enchanting Bonfire Effect that has the power to draw people in, and in others, I find spent malls that lost their spark long ago. Resurrecting the vitality of malls isn't as simple as conducting a cosmetic makeover and upgrading materials. It requires rethinking the unique value malls can add to people's lives, revisiting the question of what problems they solve for society, and repositioning their meaning, identity, and purpose in the consumer's mind.

Since culture and place are my business, I learn from both successful and failed malls equally. But I don't have to travel far to find solid examples because within a three-mile radius of my home in Los Angeles, I have four excellent case studies that provide tremendous insights for anyone involved in place-making and place-management.

Three of these shopping centers—Century City Mall, Beverly Center, and Ovation Hollywood (formerly Hollywood & Highland)—were built decades ago and have endured several major renovations and repositioning attempts. Some of these overhauls eclipsed the billion-dollar mark to appeal to the public's ever-changing tastes and escape the stigma of being labeled a "mall," which is no longer as desirable of a term as it once was. Yet if you ask the average consumer today what these three places are, as we regularly do at our firm, they'll look at you dumbfounded and say, "Uhh . . . they're malls!" They react this way because, in their eyes, the "form and shape"—a topic we'll discuss further in chapter five—of these places still look, feel, and operate like traditional malls.

The fourth place near my home is not a traditional mall per se, even though it has similar tenants and the same target audience; it's an internationally famous outdoor shopping center called The Grove. With a mix of old-world European street charm combined with the American main street sentimentality of a classic movie like *Miracle on 34th Street*, more than twenty million people each year visit this place (excluding the pandemic period). That's more visitors than Disneyland or the Great Wall of China! It's one of the most successful shopping center developments in the U.S., yet at $160 million to build, it cost a fraction of the other three major malls near it, designed by world-renowned architecture firms.

So what's so special about The Grove? What does Rick Caruso, the rockstar developer of this highly sought-after destination, know that the international developers and world-famous architects don't? And how has The Grove maintained its appeal for decades in a city where "coolness" changes faster than Kim Kardashian's wardrobe?

In a word: *escapism*.

HOW TO ESCAPE L.A.

I love L.A.! It's a fabulous city full of great people, food, art, culture, weather, and diversity. But it's also a big city with big-city realities and challenges—such as traffic, pollution, crime, homelessness, high cost of living, and a severe housing crisis—that are hard to wrap your head around some days, much less solve. As the largest county in the U.S., with over ten million residents, it's easy to get lost here, literally and figuratively. Many people who live in, work in, and visit

L.A. can find themselves yearning for that sense of community, neighborliness, and connectedness to others we all know exists somewhere out there but can't seem to find except for in little pockets of paradise in the city.

While most people know The Grove is not a real, historic downtown but a manufactured stage set, it's fun to escape from the realities of life and be someone else for a while, even if it's only a few hours of "make-believe." Although the place might be "fake," the emotions and behaviors of how people respond in the place are real.

But it's not just the residents of L.A. who need to escape the realities of life; whether we live in Manhattan, Milwaukee, or Missoula, we all need to take a break from ourselves, our jobs, and the overwhelming complexity of the world some days. Escapism, fantasy, acting out other sides of our persona, and indulging our imagination muscles are effective strategies for coping with stress and better understanding ourselves, what we want out of life, and what makes us happy. Much as we get to see and experience the lives of other people, places, and times through books, movies, and vacations, we can also do the same through places as long as they can keep us engaged and engrossed in an imaginative story of the place, which The Grove does exceptionally well.

The idea of indulging "consumer fantasies" and creating "places of imagination" upsets some designers as not real or cerebral enough for them. But so many things we buy and places we frequent are not real, such as that reassembled Irish pub in Omaha, Nebraska, the four-wheel-drive Land Rover we drive only on city streets that never touches a grain of sand, the French Tudor home we hope to live in someday, or that African safari vacation we dream of taking. These places and products represent symbols and icons of a fantasy lifestyle that we use to indulge our dreams and differentiate ourselves from others. And for millions of people, The Grove epitomizes an imaginative place they would like to be in or at least have access to from time to time as one aspect of their persona.

The mistake I see many malls make is trying to be "trendy," "cultured," and intellectually "with it." While these well-designed venues might be aesthetically interesting to look at, they're far too conscious and do little to put visitors into an imaginative state or allow them to dream or enter a fantasy persona. The hallmark of a great designer is someone who can transport us to another place. However, the three malls I mentioned at the outset of this chapter have no recognizable place, era, or story-world they wish us to enter. Instead, they ask visitors to appreciate their surroundings as if they were admiring an abstract painting they don't entirely understand or relate to in a modern museum. Customers don't think of them as a form of escape as much as they do a place to purchase products in a deliberate, conscious manner.

Whenever my clients visit our L.A. office, we take them to The Grove to learn more about "consumer fantasies" and "places of imagination" that naturally reside in people's collective consciousness. Teaching this subject at The Grove, however, isn't difficult because the crowd's palpable energy and the social behaviors they reveal are self-evident, if not intoxicating. Whether my clients sell motorcycles, housewares, or turkey burgers, they always walk away from The Grove with a free education on how to tap into the imaginative side of consumers and give them a taste of social bliss they'll crave indulging in often. I can't tell you the number of game-changing ideas this 365-day learning lab has sparked for my clients and staff, such as a motorcycle village for bikers in Florida, a new farmers market stall format for a grocery store chain in Illinois, and a high-volume kiosk program for an urban park in L.A. But before we get too far into these techniques, let's first define what an experience is.

As I define it, an experience is close to the state of awe in that it can shift our attention away from ourselves and make us feel like we're a part of something bigger. The best experiences allow us to forget time, taxes, and the tediousness of life, which is a desirable state of mind to escape to from time to time. The right experience creates a resonance between ourselves and our environment and can make us feel more generous, friendly, and connected to others in our environment. When we find ourselves enraptured by the experience of a great place, it's as if we've entered an altered state of flow that transcends the mundaneness of everyday life. And who doesn't want to feel that way every so often?

The Grove offers an encyclopedic set of tips, tools, and techniques for creating an immersive experience and understanding the critical components of fostering prosocial behaviors. But if there are two lessons and critical skills I want my clients to learn from the developer Rick Caruso and his team to bring back to their organizations and incorporate into their place strategy, they would be the following:

First, Caruso zeroes in on what people feel they are missing in their lives and fills that void.

Second, he's obsessive about ensuring that each step in the customer journey has a payoff that outweighs the perceived work required.

FILLING THE VOID

Everyone in business wants to know, "What's new?" But a better question for creating new market opportunities is to ask, "What's missing?"

One of the major voids we see across demographics—from the Ernies of the world approaching retirement to the recent college graduates trying to find their place in society—is people's need and desire to make good friends, feel less isolated and lonely, and belong to something more meaningful.

Most of us know what we need to do to feel less alone. Get offline and go outside to see what's happening in our community. We can join a bowling league or book club, take up a new sport or join an art class. But making new friends and feeling a sense of belonging isn't easy in this era of worry and suspicion. The Grove allows us to fill that void for free without a steep initial hurdle. We can access that sense of belonging and meaning by merely walking on the property and falling into the natural flow of human synchronicity of people meandering around The Grove without instructions or worry about fitting in, as we can all find our natural place and rhythm there. The place makes it safe to say hello to people and strike up a casual conversation with strangers. I'm not suggesting people replace the bowling league or art classes with The Grove—as I believe wholeheartedly in the community-making benefits of those activities. But if we need a quick shot of social connection and a healthy dose of feel-good community spirit, this is the place where it can happen without exerting much effort.

The architectural critics will pick me apart for having the audacity to talk about the sense of community happening at a shopping center, heaven forbid. But I'm not the person they should argue with; they should aim their complaints at the millions of annual visitors, who they often describe as "unrefined" and "lacking sophisticated taste."

What's remarkable about The Grove is that it does the seemingly impossible job of attracting three different audience profiles that, in most developments, usually chase each other off—locals, hipsters, and tourists. These three ships pass in the night without knocking each other off course. Interestingly enough, though, the moment they leave the property, they resort back to horn honking and bird-flipping, demonstrating a central point of this book about how much a place's environment affects people's behavior and willingness to cooperate with others in a prosocial manner. Curiously, these three ships don't frequent The Grove because they're dying to buy T-shirts at the Gap, khakis at the Banana Republic, or running shoes at the Nike store. One can find those items anywhere, cheaper, faster, and with less effort. The unique product people desire to acquire at The Grove is a shared social experience and a sense of community, which so much of modern life lacks, particularly in car-dependent cities like L.A.

Rather than creating something new and futuristic—which so many in business and design circles chase—Caruso restores something familiar from the past wisdom of our ancestors that people feel is missing in their lives today. A 2013 *Vanity Fair* article summed up this point nicely, quoting Caruso as saying, "It was very important for me to try to *transport* people to a better place and time. I wanted to create a Main Street for a city that does not have one. Each element of the Grove is engineered to bring a sense of security and a feeling of familiarity that verges on nostalgia." The article continues, saying, "Caruso's street features a trolley car and connects to the old Farmers Market, all of which seems to link it to an innocent L.A. past." While "innocence" may not be the first word that comes to mind when people think of L.A. today, what makes the idea so compelling is how effectively it restores something people feel is lost in the city's massive scale but found in the quaint main street at The Grove.

Despite its apparent success and undeniable attraction, the architectural critics and intellectual elites deride The Grove as "imitation," "not inventive enough," and "too derivative," which are the most lethal of all architectural insults for designers to hear from their priestly guild. (But can you imagine if your doctor didn't want to perform a proven surgery because it was "too derivative" and not "inventive" enough?) This intellectual critique of The Grove speaks to how architects view their job, if not life's purpose, as ordained artists creating original works of art instead of studying the time-tested principles of what's worked for communities and towns for hundreds, if not thousands, of years. The Grove doesn't aim to appease the highbrow tastes of designers but focuses on creating community bliss and a social respite for the rest of us.

Is The Grove cute, syrupy, and quaint? Absolutely! But when people naturally gravitate to a place, it says something about what the culture seeks, what kind of environments resonate with the public, and what course corrections they'd like to see in the future. Designers can debate whether The Grove is "good architecture"—frankly, I'm not a fan of the design style—but that's missing the point. The Grove, as my business partner and planning expert, Terry Shook, taught me, is just good urban planning, outdoor room design, and social convening. It's not about the buildings but the social life, connections, and behaviors that happen between these structures.

As fascinating as The Grove is, is it a perfect model for convening people? No. I wish it embraced the exterior streets better and included more diverse housing, office, and institutional uses and audiences outside retail and food. But despite these drawbacks, The Grove consistently delivers an emotional payoff and social reward for those desperately seeking to be around other humans in a safe, friendly, and prosocial environment.

LESS WORK, MORE PAYOFF

When evaluating the experience places offer, my team and I consider two broad categories:

- moments and situations that feel like work, effort, and exertion
- moments and situations that feel like joy, delight, and rejuvenation

We call this dynamic the "work/payoff ratio," or "WPR" for short.

When people consider visiting a mall, furniture store, art museum, theme park, or any other place, they subconsciously ask themselves, "If I go through the effort to visit this place, what's in it for me? I can see how the place wins by getting me on their premise, but how do I win by going there?" Far too many place-based businesses and institutions I study are unsympathetic about the effort required for consumers to acquire a venue's product. But to succeed in today's digital alternative world, places must gain clarity on this subconscious work/payoff dynamic to ensure their moments of pleasure far outweigh their pain points.

Once we achieve the right balance of the work/payoff ratio, we focus on ensuring our client's "experience" stands out in the marketplace as distinctly different and "worth the trip" from all the other competitive alternatives. Most businesses use the classic term "value proposition" to define their offering. However, we believe it's essential for places today to develop a compelling "experience value proposition," or "EVP" for short. We define and use this EVP to ensure everyone on the team recognizes that the *experience* of their place is a core part of their offering, not a side issue, an afterthought, or a nice-to-have layer sprinkled on top of the value proposition.

When analyzing places, we use the WPR and the EVP as a framework to help evaluate, clarify, and position what we're offering the public in a way that immediately allows them to see what they can do there and how they'll win if they visit our client's venue. We give ourselves around two seconds to communicate that value to consumers, which is about the same time people glance at a movie poster to decide whether they have an interest in seeing the film or not. (We'll discuss the power of the movie poster technique to sharpen your core offering in more detail in chapter nine.)

Perhaps unconsciously, Caruso masters these equations of the "work required" and the "experience offered" better than any developer in the industry. He understands the importance of evaluating every single step of the customer journey to ensure the payoff and reward are head and shoulders above the perceived work they have to endure to engage with the place.

When visiting a mall, there are a host of seemingly "small" annoying aspects that subconsciously discourage most people from wanting to make the trip. These hassles might include navigating parking, finding a clean bathroom, using escalators, waiting for elevators, and making their way from one end of the property to the other in their attempt to find what they are looking to purchase. Caruso took all these hurdles and pain points and turned them into first-class experiences.

As a psychological principle, how a place starts and finishes sets the tone for that place's overall experience, memory, and recall. Get this right, and you'll be light-years ahead of the competition, yet those are the specific things that most malls, and other places, miss so terribly, even when their data tells them how important they are to customers. But Caruso starts and ends the experience of his place on high notes that don't detour customer visits, but encourage them as easy enticements and distinctive moments.

The unique experience of visiting The Grove starts in the parking decks, escalators, and elevators, which provide great aerial views, music from the moment you open your car door (think Sinatra with a dash of the trolley car and bells chiming in), lights, red carpet, and captivating billboards of celebrities and affirmational messages highlighting The Grove's primary offerings. Like the processional forecourt to a castle, the fun starts even before you arrive, and the joy still resonates on your way out.

Once you're "on the lot," you're met with a concierge area reminiscent of a 5-star hotel lobby. To the right of this arrival feature, if you can take your eyes off or hold your kids back from running toward the water fountain that dances in step with Sinatra's voice, you'll see bathrooms that made the finalists for the best bathrooms in the country. Sharply dressed bathroom attendants, hand towels, high-end fragrant soap brands and mouthwash, fresh-cut flowers, and aromatic smells provide a sharp contrast to the typical mall bathroom experience of a) having trouble finding it and b) walking down a white-walled corridor past stock rooms and janitor closets only to find prison-like, vandal-proof bathrooms that make people feel dirtier than when they entered.

Mall developers know that customers loathe the traditional bathroom experiences in their facilities. But because of their lack of focus on the work/payoff ratio and development of a compelling experience value proposition, the bathrooms typically get the back-of-house spaces and secondary treatment, not the priority design placement or thinking. But Caruso understands the importance of how the most intimate spaces leave an indelible impression on customers that stick in their minds as generous and hospitable.

No detail is overlooked or too small to improve at The Grove. If you want to take a break, there is plenty of lawn space to have a picnic, and if you forgot a blanket, no problem. The Grove has you covered with free, clean blankets. Even the security guards project friendliness and promote social experiences. Rather than looking like the "truancy police" chasing down teens on Segways in traditional malls, at The Grove, they wear sport coats like porters or butlers. Just by observing them, it's clear they view their job as a way to support their guests' experiences by being promoters of good times rather than enforcers of rules.

While L.A. is an uber-progressive city, Caruso isn't trying to be cutting-edge or build an egotistical monument to himself. Instead, he uncovers what people are missing in their lives and fills those voids with some of the best qualities of the past they yearn for, providing them with a payoff that outweighs the perceived work required. The success of The Grove is plain to see in the number of visitors, prosocial behaviors, and remarkable success of stores there.

But that said, what can something like a local grocery store chain trying to keep its doors open as national and international retailers siphon off their customers learn from the experience offered by The Grove? Let's find out.

WHEN THE INTERNATIONAL GIANTS TOOK OVER THE LOCAL MAIN STREET

There was a time when local grocery stores were the unsung heroes of their towns. The owners raised their families in these communities and knew their customers and their kids on a first-name basis. Their money came from the community and went right back into it through local jobs, local causes, and local investments.

But then, the national and international chains came to town.

Their shock and awe retail weaponry, advanced data analytics, and immense investment capacity allowed their cost of doing business to be light-years ahead of what the local operators could achieve. However, instead of crushing the local stores in one fell swoop, which wouldn't go over well in the community, the giants surrounded the local operators' brand fortress on the town's suburban perimeter and beltways. Over time, they disrupted their supply chain networks through greater negotiation leverage and waited for them to come out into the open battlefield to compete on price, variety, and convenience so they could expose how much the local chains charged for commodity products like Tide detergent, Crest toothpaste, and Cheerios cereal. This one-two punch combo of pressure and patience was a brilliant strategy. It allowed the giants to seize large swaths of the retail landscape across North America with the massive funding of Wall Street's war chest and their insistence on growth and expansion at all costs.

When I met the Lovsin family, owners of the Alberta, Canada–based grocery store chain Freson Bros. in 2010, they found themselves in the crosshairs of national and international retailers infiltrating their territory.

I've worked with many family businesses in my career, but the Lovsin family were some of the most wholesome, decent, and caring folks I'd ever met in the grocery industry. Frank Lovsin, the founder, and his wife, Agnes, were both proud children of new immigrants to Canada. The loving couple carried from their European heritage a long line of family values, food traditions, and a humble work ethic that radiated throughout their entire family.

Like many local chains at the time, Freson Bros., founded in 1955, was in the midst of improving and "professionalizing" their stores, which is to say, rather than lean into their homespun qualities, they tried to catch up to and imitate the best practices and sophisticated techniques of the national and international chains. Ironically enough, this is exactly what their competitors wanted them to do. What's hard to see in the fog of war, though, is that they'd never beat the retail giants at their preferred game of price, variety, and convenience. If anything, local chains that tried this approach only flattered the giants' business models while diluting the uniqueness of their own brand.

Freson patrolled their territory vigilantly and polished their store operations meticulously, but they went into daily battle using outdated store design strategies. While this approach might've worked well in the 1990s, it's not enough to survive the firestorm of latest techniques the retail giants can hurl their way today. I know this because my team and I worked for those giants and developed many of those lethal techniques for them.

My first objective with Freson was to keep them from entering that bloody battlefield frontally. My second objective was to convince them to build an entirely new store format to more nimbly navigate the changing competitive terrain and capture consumer interest with human drivers such as family values, the craft of food traditions, and social proof of the power of community—which the Lovsin family had in spades. Rather than ask consumers what they want, as far too many retailers do, I wanted Freson to step back into their family roots and double down on their folksy values to impose their wholesome view on the world.

But we couldn't just put the words "family," "craft," and "community" on signs and expect the masses to follow their flag. Instead, we needed to drill into what those "meanings" meant and how customers could taste, touch, and feel them within the store experience. To extract these qualities, we spent a lot of time with the Lovsin family, not only in their stores but also in their homes and even at The Grove in L.A.

THE LOVSIN FAMILY VISITS L.A.

When the Lovsin family arrived at The Grove, I watched them pull off their professional business masks and slip into their imaginative human selves, as I've seen so many clients do. As excited as they were to get out of our office after a long day of strategic design presentations, I knew they were wondering what in the heck visiting a shopping center had to do with helping them stave off the national and international competitors breathing down their necks.

I let them ponder that question as we walked around The Grove because sometimes it's more illuminating to "feel" great retail with your feet, eyes, ears, and nose than to "think" about it analytically like a calculus problem. But the dots didn't fully connect until Frank Lovsin stepped into the Original Farmers Market zone attached to The Grove.

Mesmerized by the imperfect wooden stall construction, handwritten signs, and old-fashioned merchandising techniques, he realized the uber-hip city of L.A. finds county fair–like stalls cool and desirable. And while holding a bag of homemade caramel popcorn from a local merchant, a light bulb went off. "We can do this!" he declared to his management team as he took in the atmosphere around him that reminded him of his small-town roots. "By God, we can do this better than anyone because it's who we are by nature."

This spark of creativity by the Lovsin family of seeing their future found in their past was powerful to witness. Combine this with the Lovsins gaining the confidence to bet on themselves when seeing how The Grove beat the Goliaths of the shopping industry by not being futuristic but traditional and by offering a one-of-a-kind experience value proposition, and the management team was eager to approve our new store design and brand strategy.

As helpful as The Grove field trip was, though, we still had our work cut out for us. We still had to figure out how to manifest the wholesome values the Lovsins represented into tangible benefits their customers could grasp immediately and feel within two seconds of walking into their stores. But this time, the spark of creativity would come from visiting their home turf.

HOME IS WHERE THE BIG IDEAS RESIDE

Designers and consultants are surprised to learn my team and I regularly ask our clients if we can visit their homes. But few places in life reveal what matters most to a leader than the comfort and intimacy of their homes.

When I entered Frank and Agnes's lovely but modest home, I saw a treasure trove of artifacts and biographical materials pointing to things they deeply cared about. Among the many photos, one black-and-white picture on the wall caught my eye the most. It showed a young man in a white apron holding a pair of meat cleavers. When I asked Frank about the image, he told us a captivating story of starting his career as a butcher in a coal mining town and explained how few working in grocery stores today understand what being a butcher is anymore. He spoke about it as if it was a lost art, which got my wheels spinning.

Upon entering their kitchen, Agnes told us a heartwarming story about how her mother taught her to make apple strudel dough so clear you could read a newspaper underneath. When we sat to eat dinner, I noticed the clean, white porcelain dishes and the delicate but simple lace tablecloth from Europe, where their families originated and they regularly visited. While ornate, these elements weren't showy, extravagant, or ostentatious but had a purity that felt wholesome and comforting. The meal consisted of savory deli meats, homemade bread, and a delectable array of condiments and fixings. While we ate, Frank and Agnes told memorable stories about how they survived long, dark winters and economic hard times by preserving and canning healthy fruits, vegetables, and soups in curated mason jars and storing them in root cellars.

Everything about the Lovsins' narrative revolved around family values, sticking together, bonding over meals, and respecting the craft of where good food comes from. What they cared about most and devoted their lives to was what many of their hardworking customers cared about and aspired to achieve in their families' lives. But these good values weren't just sentimental feelings; there was real wisdom and solid advice on eating and living better and the essential ingredients for raising healthy families.

Much like the moment when Frank grabbed the bag of homemade caramel popcorn at The Grove, sitting around that table and listening to the Lovsins talk passionately about their heritage and traditions, I had a light-bulb moment of my own. My team and I realized everything we needed to expand Freson's value equation and beat the retail giants was right there in their home, their values, and their way of thinking about how food convenes families in meaningful ways. As a result, we designed a store that manifested those qualities in tangible form and experience.

THE PROOF IS IN THE PUDDING

Thus far, we've built several new prototype stores for Freson Bros., all of which are revolutionizing their business and markets, and we have more ambitious new stores on the way. The chain has won several distinguished awards, including the Independent Grocer of the Year by the Canadian Federation of Independent Grocers (CFIG), the highest national industry award recognizing the success of outstanding independent retailers. And while writing this book, Freson won the 2022 national gold award for large format store by CFIG, getting us closer to our dream goal of making Freson the Wegmans of the Great White North.

Today the chain is on fire and winning local customers' hearts, minds, and spirits. But these victories aren't because they tried to play the retail giants' traditional game of price, variety, and convenience. Their triumph is because they expanded the grocery store value equation to include other human qualities and concerns customers care about acquiring in their lives.

Based on our visit and conversations in the Lovsin family home, we designed and developed a root cellar, a customer favorite and frequent talking point. We created a new beef program/department and a private label brand, Real Alberta Beef, featuring proprietary meats from their territory focused on the "lost art of butchery." And to show how serious the Lovsin family is about meat, we designed a sensory-rich area in the meat department called Banj's Smokehouse, named after Frank Lovsin's brother, who loves to smoke meat. You can't walk into that part of the store without smelling and seeing the fresh cuts of meat through the showcase windows. We designed a health and beauty zone in the store called Grandma Cures, which came from conversations with Doug Lovsin's wife, Deanna, who told us about the homeopathic ways her family treated health issues.

But we didn't stop with our initial concept, as Frank's sons—Mike, Doug, and Ken—are determined to push the envelope to continually give their community the best of what they've got. While designing a recent prototype direction, a whopper of a surprise breakthrough arose. The CEO, Doug Lovsin, hired a new bread expert, Jay Cummings, who quit his high-paying job for one of the retail giants because they wanted him to develop a program to create bread products that would last on the shelf for twenty-one days. This request violated Jay's bread-making values and ethics, so he joined forces with Freson. When Doug told us about Jay, we worked with them to develop two new branded departments in the store—Mother Dough Bread Co. and Father Dough Pizza—which are the exact opposite of the unnatural, flavorless "twenty-one-day bread" as they revere the old-world craft of bread-making. These two concepts have put Freson on not just the local map but the national map and set the pace for exemplifying Freson's passion for respecting the craft of food.

Freson is the real deal. Their community knows it, and customers quickly grasp it. The new brand mantra we developed with them—"Handled with Care"—entails zero fluff; it's obvious to anyone who walks into their stores that they have the utmost respect for their products, their providers, their team, and their community. When something is true, it resonates deeply with people. And all of this newfound momentum kicked off with Frank reaching for a bag of homemade caramel popcorn at The Grove and having the audacity to head in the opposite direction of the industry.

It'd be easy to read these "David vs. Goliath" stories and draw the conclusion that, "Okay, all I need to do is embrace the past, and I can carve my own future." But that would be missing the point. Both Caruso of The Grove and the Lovsin family of Freson uncovered what was missing in their communities and then mustered the courage to tell the world what they cared about, which just happened to be what customers cared about too. And then they executed their experience value proposition with precision as their experience became an essential part of their product offering.

THE FUTURE LIES IN IRREPLACEABLE PLACES

The decision to visit a place entails more work than ordering from Amazon or Postmates. There's no denying it. You have to put on presentable clothes, drive a car, find parking, navigate crowds, and hope the bathroom line isn't too long and the toilets come with a seat. The truth is places require a higher caloric expenditure, which the technology companies call friction. But visionaries like Rick Caruso of The Grove and Frank Lovsin of Freson look at friction points as opportunities to create an irreplaceable experience.

Turning this friction into experiential opportunities requires having a microscopic focus on the work/payoff ratio and an awareness of what kind of experience value proposition your target audience would find "worth the trip."

To withstand the forces of change barreling down on us today, rather than thinking of your place as a "store," "facility," or "warehouse," think of it as a performing arts center akin to something like Cirque du Soleil, whose job is to attract audiences daily to their theatrical shows. This engaging show must be an irreplaceable human experience worth the price of admission that online providers can't replicate. Going to see Cirque du Soleil requires a certain amount of work, effort, and energy, but it comes with emotional, social, and sensory rewards and payoffs you can't get anywhere else.

The brilliance of both The Grove and Freson Bros. is that they ask themselves: "How can we ensure our guests have a physical, social, and emotional experience that transcends the work required to acquire our offering and provides a payoff that can't be found elsewhere, including online?" Not many mall executives think to this degree of specificity across each critical human dimension. If they did, they wouldn't tolerate an exhausting parking experience or a less than stellar bathroom experience, as the competitor malls entail. And even fewer leaders in the retail and grocery industry pass this test. But to stand out today, it's wise not to look through the same frame as most competitors.

In Part III of this book, we'll dive into how to create consumer fantasies and places of imagination in more detail. But first, before thinking about design, we need a better understanding of how places influence human behaviors, perceptions, and decisions.

Note: Sadly, during the writing of this book, Frank Lovsin, the founder of Freson Bros., passed away at the age of eighty-eight. When I think about the greatest leaders and role models in my life, Frank ranks high on the list. His unshakable belief in the power of community and his insistence on treating everyone in your sphere as part of your family left a profound mark on me and my colleagues. We all looked to him as a father figure and fountain of wisdom. He exemplified what it means to be irreplaceable. Fortunately, though, there is a long line of well-trained Lovsin family members to carry on his loving legacy.

PART TWO

Under the Radar of Consciousness: How Places Influence Our Behaviors in Ways We Don't Always See

"The real voyage of discovery lies not in seeking new landscapes but in seeing with new eyes."

—Marcel Proust

AFTER A GOOD NIGHT'S REST, most of us wake up feeling like a fully charged electric vehicle. But to give ourselves an extra boost before hitting the road, we throw back a cup of coffee to turbocharge the tank. As we go about our day—navigating meetings, tackling assignments, and running into a maze of detours, dead ends, and roadblocks—we look for small breaks to recharge with snacks and idle chitchat with colleagues about the weather, sports, or the latest TV series. But after a quick pit stop, we put the pedal to the metal again, pushing our bodies and minds to the redline.

By the end of the workday, we can feel our body's batteries wearing down, our mental performance waning, and our ability to take on more tasks fading. But as we head out of work, our spouse calls and asks, "Honey, do you mind dropping by the grocery store to pick up a few things?" This slight detour almost causes us to blow a gasket because we barely have enough energy to make it home, much less take on the grocery store obstacle course.

While many of us can relate to this scenario, the people in charge of designing and managing places assume we come to their venues fully charged and raring to go. They forget we don't have an unlimited energy supply and overlook the body's fuel we've already spent powering through our day. The last thing we want to endure is the aggravation of circling the parking lot, the mental calculus of searching for pimento cheese, and waiting in long, annoying lines.

Everything we do on an average day—from getting the kids ready for school, talking on the phone with vendors, interacting with coworkers in meetings, responding to emails, and, yes, going to the grocery store—consumes our body's precious energy supply. And everything we encounter in our environment, from stoplights to deli department signage, solicits our body's attention and processing power—but there's only so much focus we can give them.

As humans, we have a finite amount of energy to tackle our day, deal with roadblocks, and digest the barrage of information around us before reaching a point where we can't go any further without recharging. If forced to keep going, we can become irritable, impatient, and ineffective, which my team and I frequently observe in stores as exhausted customers wait in line during rush-hour shopping.

But let's flip the last-minute spouse request around another way.

What if your spouse called to see if you wanted to take a walk in the park after work or enjoy a relaxing meal and glass of wine at your favorite patio café instead of trekking through grocery store aisles? Your body's tank would naturally fill up with energy and make you feel restored, not drained.

Why is that?

Because some places, situations, and moments in life have the capacity to recharge our batteries and fill our tanks with energy. They create visually, sensually, and experientially harmonious environments that make visiting them feel like pleasure, not work. The sensory stimulation they provide doesn't require thinking, calculating, or decoding to make sense of. Instead of inducing a state of visual chaos or disorganization, they provide a sense of visual resolution that is comforting to the eyes and calming to the soul. As experience designers, our goal is to transform as many battery-draining places as possible into human recharging stations.

ATTENTION, AWARENESS, AND CONSCIOUSNESS

Designing places and experiences that fill people with energy requires understanding how the human body, mind, and senses operate under the radar of our consciousness. For instance, we don't tell ourselves when to breathe or blink or how to walk. These things happen automatically on a subconscious level, as do many of our other behaviors, movements, and actions in the physical world.

I recognize that "consciousness" is one of those fuzzy words that scientists and yoga teachers can't agree on, but for our purposes, I am referring to two critical human factors: attention and awareness. While these faculties are intertwined, attention monitors our environment, whereas awareness pulls things out of the background for us to focus on briefly. Of course, there are times when we notice things in our environment on a more conscious, rational level. Most of the time, though, we're not fully aware of what sensory stimuli grab our attention, as our bodies make all kinds of reflexive decisions on a subconscious level. My team and I are most interested in understanding these attention-grabbing stimuli and subconscious decision-making systems because they help explain human behavior and allow us to design places that have the power to convene people.

One would assume that the fields of design and retail would make learning how these human systems work mandatory reading, but there is little education, much less awareness, on these topics in business or design school. Most designers I encounter fixate on overtly conscious design aspects, not the subconscious processes for how humans interpret spaces through their senses. On the other hand, most executives I meet are hard-core disciples of numerical data and see their world through the lens of a spreadsheet rather than the eyes of the average human being. They obsess over "always having the right item in stock at just the right time." What they fail to see, however, is that without foot traffic and visual engagement, they've got no shot at making the sale.

To help arm clients with the fundamental principles of how customers perceive, experience, and catalog their stores, we created a course entitled Behavioral Design Series. This course teaches retail leaders, managers, and frontline staff how humans make sense of their environments to create better experiences that fill consumers' tanks with energy and enthusiasm.

The following four chapters highlight the primary frames through which we can see human behaviors exhibited in everyday situations.

- The first frame describes the critical role the senses play in helping us navigate our world.

- The second frame highlights the difference between a utilitarian approach to place design versus a more emotive approach before diving into the ideal state consumers wish to be in, which I call the "Dream of Someday."

- The third frame will shed light on the standard "forms and shapes" that make up our world and the predictive coding systems humans use to quickly determine what an object or place is about.

- And the last frame discusses the ability to command an audience's attention by crafting deliberate scenes that elicit specific emotions and create a collective group experience.

When pulled together, these four frames allow us to see the world through a new perspective far more influential and meaningful than the traditional laws of architectural aesthetics.

Making "Sense" of Place

*"All our knowledge begins with the senses, proceeds
then to understanding, and ends with reasoning."*
—Immanuel Kant

HERE'S MY TYPICAL WEEK: I fly across the country, pick up my rental car, and drive to a manicured corporate campus before walking into a conference room where I'm immediately met with the backsides of two dozen formally dressed executives and dapper designers huddled over a table.

What are they looking at?

The immaculately conceived floor plan we've been working on for months.

This passionate group of Capitalists and Creators moves pieces around the large drawings spread out before them like military generals mapping out an invasion strategy. They haggle over department sizes, locations, adjacencies, and linear shelf space and debate every inch of the store with the same concentration and suspense as you'd see at a craps table in Vegas. However, the stakes in this game aren't someone's pocket change but the capital budget allocations of a large corporation. Make this bet wrong and you could lose the company millions and be out on the street looking for a new job.

I've witnessed this scene and participated in this floor plan design ritual over a thousand times in my career. My first boss drilled into me the importance of getting this divinely inspired floor plan perfect. And my clients reinforced this practice by spending a whopping amount of time setting up lengthy review meetings, formal leadership presentations, and endless follow-up calls to adjust these documents.

But why the fixation?

Floor plans enable designers and managers to get a bird's-eye view of the store, allowing them to see the entirety of the departments, aisles, and back-of-house areas in one glance. While this overview is a useful and necessary part of the process, floor plans laid out horizontally on a table have one big problem: unless someone is sixty feet tall, they don't represent how customers visually grasp, digest, or experience a grocery store. Not even close.

To see this in action, let's look through the eyes of how Darcy Williams, from Carlisle, Pennsylvania, sees the average grocery store versus how the operators and designers lay them out.

Unlike store designers, Darcy doesn't see her local grocery store from a bird's-eye view. Instead, she walks upright and forward with the intent to "get the job done" as quickly and painlessly as possible. The shelves are all taller than Darcy's five-foot, five-inch frame, affording her only partial snippets of the store from her viewpoint. Her eyes prefer to look straight ahead as she pushes her awkward cart because it's not easy or natural for her to crank her head and neck from left to right to look at both sides of the aisle simultaneously to find the products on the crumpled-up list in her hand. As a result, her body and mind constantly have to work and make split-second choices about what sides of the aisle to look at and how much of the shelf lineup and packaging information to study in detail. Not to mention making room for other customers with shopping carts and equally hurried mindsets approaching her from all directions.

There's a reason media companies place billboards on the highways at an angle. If they ran these marketing signs parallel to the street, we'd wreck our cars while trying to turn our necks 180 degrees to read them all. Despite this, we ask and expect shoppers to do this every day when walking down most grocery store aisles.

How did we end up with these long, parallel aisle configurations that don't work well for the human body and eyes? And why does this uncomfortable pattern persist?

The rise of the supermarket concept took place in an era when getting products to far-off communities and then onto shelves in the right quantity at the right price was an exciting but ambitious undertaking. Leaders didn't have time to worry about human comfort as much as they had to focus on product availability. Because of the scale of this operation, organizations had to invest heavily in supply-side systems and logistical thinkers to figure out how to get all 40,000–60,000-plus products from the fields and factories to the warehouse, off the truck, out of the shipping boxes, into refrigerated cases, and onto the shelves neat, straight, and priced right each day.

The supply process is much easier today because of the sophisticated tools and technological advances of automation. But yet, many stores still have a warehouse mentality of uncomfortable inventoried aisles that make the operator's jobs easier but not that of the customer. This inconvenience was tolerable when there was more customer demand for stores than the supply of stores and products. Today, however, we live in an over-stored era, where consumers have a glut of brick-and-mortar stores as well as online product options. The challenge for physical retailers moving forward is creating sufficient consumer demand and desire for their store experiences. This realization should translate into less uncomfortable stores and a more enjoyable shopping experience for the customer.

But this isn't always the case.

If we designed stores for the ease and comfort of customers, we wouldn't have so many aisles because long, narrow aisles (or alleys or corridors) are not places humans like to be. Instead, we'd design rooms in the store—even if they're "implied" or "perceptual rooms," as we call them in our firm, defined by the ceiling, floor, or low wall treatments—based on mindset/solution zones, such as healthy eating, holiday planning, and preparing school lunches.

Like the checkout zone, grocery aisles are just one of many standard spatial configurations of the past that retailers keep forcing customers to endure even though they are not the most comfortable environments for humans to be in. Instead of accepting the standard grocery store chassis as is, the future winners in the grocery industry will be the ones who put the customer's comfort, convenience, body mechanics, and experience first over that of supply logistics.

To date, the operational logistics of grocery store layouts have won out over the human senses and customer comfort. But this operator-first mentality will someday change abruptly for retailers, just as it did for taxis and many other industries, because if this era is about anything, it's about removing friction, discomfort, and frustrations. Before Uber rode into town, we all had to accept the taxi industry paradigm "as is," complete with rude drivers, uncomfortable seats, unsavory sounds and smells, and an archaic payment system. While the taxi industry was well aware of the customer's dislike of these uncomfortable situations, they got away with it because there were no other options. But a small upstart with no experience in transportation changed all that by removing the frustrations and discomfort of taxis and turning million-dollar taxi medallions into worthless investments. I fear this same attrition will happen to resistant-to-change grocery stores.

When I work with grocery leaders, they're fine with my team changing the pinstriping and decor of the store vehicle. Some of the more progressive ones will even allow us to change the body style and contours of the store departments. But few will allow us to touch, much less change, the underlying chassis of the store, which for the last sixty years consisted of the same configuration of aisles, center store, perimeter, and checkout zone. When my team and I suggest getting rid of some aisles and moving the checkout area to a different location instead of the malfunction junction scenario that currently exists with long aisles dead-ending into a jam-packed checkout zone, the look I get from retailers screams, *These are questions we should not ask!* It's as if a design god in grocery heaven declares, *Thou shalt not change the grocery store chassis!*

If grocery stores want to survive the frictionless future of digital alternatives, they must prioritize the customer's needs, comfort, and convenience over logistics because technology is taking over the logistics game. And if store designers want to help consumers like Darcy genuinely enjoy her shopping experience, they'll have to learn more about the body mechanics of humans and how to appeal to the sensory systems of shoppers.

In the points below, you'll learn the first six principles we use to evaluate, strategize, and design the experience of places. To continue this thread of Darcy's shopping experience, I will use a typical grocery store as the primary example. Keep in mind, however, these principles apply to just about any place, environment, or experience people encounter and occupy in their day-to-day activities.

As you go over these points, you'll notice how the insights and principles overlap and bleed into each other, which is not unlike how our senses work. Our senses are not separate instruments that evaluate the contours of our environments independently or sequentially without interference from the other senses to render a final judgment. Instead, all of our senses get involved in making sense of our environment like a council of experts. For instance, when we smell something unusual, we might also hear a distant sound that notifies and informs our olfactory glands, which our eyes then confirm by noticing a shadow.

While there will be similarities from one point to the next, we'll shade them differently based on how people make sense of their environment and our desire to steer their senses and attention toward our client's offering.

1. THE VOLUNTARY VS. INVOLUNTARY EYE

While all the senses work together to help us interpret our environment, our vision plays a major role in piloting us through the world and steering our decisions in two conceptual modes: the *voluntary eye* and the *involuntary eye*. Knowing the difference between these two modes can be incredibly helpful in understanding people's engagement with their environment.

When we walk through a grocery store or any other space, our bodies let the involuntary eye "do the work" of scanning the environment and determining what to look at. Our voluntary eye doesn't get involved or engaged until something critical arises. But if we asked a computer to survey a grocery store (which is already happening in the tech world), it doesn't have a primal operating system embedded in it. These technologies don't try to interpret the subtleties and nuances of what something means. Instead, they look for trained data points, perhaps information and maybe historical knowledge, but they don't understand "meaning" because humans are the only species capable of making meaning (for now). Depending on our instructions, the computer might start from the upper left corner and move to the right to scan the entire space pixel by pixel.

Humans, however, are not linear-focused machines with an unlimited energy source. We can't afford to process every bit of data in our field of view or treat all information equally. Instead, we possess a remarkable ability to quickly assess our environment and determine the most vital bits of information to pay attention to. Our subconscious won't waste precious energy or time on the rest of the predictable, stable stuff we're already familiar with or know about from past experiences or memories. As a prediction machine, the brain constantly reconciles expectations with new information. We use our memories and senses in a two-way, elaborately networked highway of predictions, mental models, and field verification. This active predicting and sensing work tirelessly, burning up lots of energy. Which comes first—predicting or sensing?—is a matter of scientific debate, but regardless, they work in a hand-and-glove fashion to represent our world.

As part of our body's natural energy management system, we vacillate between moments of expending focused energy to look at something in detail and conserving energy by glancing past it. We subconsciously delegate those activities that aren't red alerts to our first line of defense operating system—our senses and memories—and we only send alerts to our conscious brain (the mission control center) when more visual focus, attention, or executive orders are required.

If there's too much information for the human eye to visually grasp and make sense of—as with the 40,000–60,000 items in an average grocery store—we subconsciously *goal sacrifice* and focus exclusively on the highest priority items. Even though this is good for our body's natural energy management system, it's not so good for the hardworking companies that make the products that get overlooked or bypassed by overwhelmed customers or the retailers that allocate expensive space merchandising them.

Of course, a grocery store can scream and shout at their customers with big and obnoxious yellow signage to announce their deals, but this aggressive assault only shuts down our eyes and mental processing further and drains our body's limited battery supply even more.

Despite the inherent limitations of the human body, business leaders, marketers, and designers overlook these sensory systems and visual operating issues—particularly in the totality of a store. I can't tell you the number of international consumer brand manufacturers that have shown me detailed studies of how well their multimillion-dollar product packaging redesign initiative tested in consumer surveys. What they fail to consider is that this testing is usually done with a single product on a display pedestal or screen, not in the full context of a retail store environment. The standard grocery aisle is where beautifully packaged products go to die on shelves because of drowning in an ocean of incoherent clashing visual messages.

One technique we've developed to improve the shopping experience is to give the customer's eyes something intriguing, rewarding, and coordinated with its surrounding contextual environment to look at while in the aisle. In our work for the Southern California–based grocery chain Gelson's, we designed a series of curation stations that feature gourmet products like coffee and olive oils. These perceptual zones serve as strong visual anchors in the store and provide a natural and refreshing place for the involuntary eye to rest and engage easily.

When designed in a coordinated, restrained, and evocative manner, these visual anchors don't drain our body's power but instead fills it with delight, not unlike the feeling we get when we listen to a great song while stuck in traffic on our way home from work. The same audible rhythm, harmony, hooks, and crescendos we hear in songs also apply to the visible lines, beats, rhythms, and mini-crescendo scenes we design for a grocery store aisle. And similar to how well music helps us cope with the frustrations of traffic, these visually harmonious aisles can help turn a dreaded chore into a more pleasurable shopping experience.

Can you imagine, though, if all we heard coming out of our car speakers in rush-hour traffic were clashing noises that were discordant, disharmonic, and disorganized? It would create an additional layer of distraction, confusion, and stress that would, well, drive us mad. But things get even more mentally taxing when we have to decipher highway signs at 65 mph to find the right exit ramp or seek out a particular address while having our ears bent to loud or chaotic music. Most of us immediately turn the radio down in those stressful, fast-paced situations because the human brain's capacity is limited in handling multiple demands for attention, especially if the task requires focus and concentration, such as switching multiple lanes or making a critical right turn.

Our brains have the incredible ability to switch back and forth between different tasks. But this attention-switching comes with the cost of missing things, making mistakes, and lowering our performance levels. In our desperate attempt to reduce distractions, our bodies tune out competing demands in favor of prioritizing the most urgent and critical information.

Pushing a shopping cart down an aisle is less dangerous than driving a car on a busy highway. But you can see similar customer processing challenges on full display in many retail settings where thousands of products and signs scream for our attention, toot their promotional horns, and make a lot of visual noise while failing to create an attractive, coherent tune our senses can recognize as harmonious. Humans can't handle all these incoming signals and demands for our attention when shopping, leading to mental fatigue and lower engagement with their surroundings.

2. VISUAL HARMONY VS. VISUAL NOISE

Related to the previous point, the human eye prefers "visual harmony" over "visual noise." Part of the reason for this preference is that our body's instinct, if not compulsion, is to try to make sense of an image, scene, or our surroundings.

But when we can't figure a scene or situation out because of the visual noise, our mind gets frustrated and our body's energy wears down.

Ideally, we want customers to walk into our venues feeling one way and come out a changed person with more energy and inspiration. Even though this feat may sound unattainable, we watch people come out of religious facilities, bars, concerts, Apple Stores, SoulCycle, Sender One Climbing gyms, and Harley-Davidson dealerships all the time excited by their experience and, in the best cases, with an inspired and revitalized outlook on life. For instance, I can't tell you the number of khaki-wearing business professionals who walk into a Harley store for their first time and come out wearing a leather jacket, chaps, and bandannas as they ride their new chopper off the lot to the tattoo parlor, Route 66, or a divorce lawyer. I'm exaggerating a bit for effect, but the Harley dealerships create life-changing moments for new converts daily that turn their lives around as they head off in an entirely different direction.

To feel the holy water of a brand, customers need to feel a sense of "awe" in the store and have an "experience," which must start by attracting the senses. But when the environment is too chaotic, their attention and engagement in the offering drops off significantly. We observe this daily with people going out of their way to avoid long lines, jammed-up parking spots, and crowded places. The impact of this avoidance is that we notice on average a 30 percent decline in business when construction occurs inside or outside the store. Customers subconsciously avoid these messy situations because it's hardwired in our DNA to steer clear of impediments.

However, when an object or space comes together in a visually attractive and resolved way, and everything seems balanced, well proportioned, and easy on the eyes—consumers tend to swim toward it, pay more attention to it, and engage with it more reverentially and enthusiastically, resulting in a higher level of sales lift.

One of our first priorities when redesigning a store, scene, or place is to create a visual hierarchy and logic that not only makes sense to the customer's mind in the blink of an eye but also entices them to want to engage further. Similar to how the human eye scans and reads a magazine in the order of image, headline, caption, and body of text, we can attract people's eyes through a naturally cascading, hierarchical visual logic.

Back in the '90s, the overuse of signage hit blinding levels in most grocery stores as operators couldn't resist junking up their stores with more stuff—their own and the cardboard signs, stickers, tags, banners, and promotional material that product suppliers brought into the environment. To limit this visual noise while providing our clients with a stricter design discipline and store communication approach, we developed the Seven Layers of Signage System.

1. Orientation
2. Evocative
3. Address
4. Values
5. Process
6. Promotional
7. Whisper/Nudge

To this day, we still use variations of this signage approach to help retailers clean up their act and create better store experiences that are more attractive to the human eye and less taxing on the mind and senses. In general, people interpret most spaces and places from big to small. Using the same discipline of understanding what each layer of visual design elements is for can make for a much more harmonious and pleasing shopping experience.

This visual hierarchy starts with the "orientation" and "evocative" signs that customers can see from thirty to forty feet away and goes all the way down to the three-inch level as they get closer to the products on the shelves and inside the cases, which we call the "whisper" and "nudge." Any signage that doesn't fit into one of these seven layers is deemed "visual noise," and we immediately remove it from the store.

These seven layers of communication are not inflexible and can vary per industry and audience profile. Creating an overarching organizing logic and signage system not only helps internal managers know where information goes in the store but also makes the customer's visual comprehension of the brand's complex processes more palatable and easier to digest.

3. SYMBOLS VS. WORDS

After conducting over a thousand experiential audits and space performance reviews, the most consistent mistake we see places regularly make, particularly retail stores, is where, when, and how they choose to use their words instead of symbols. While we can make out what a scene in a movie or place is about in the blink of an eye, reading sentences or words slows human processing down and requires more conscious work.

Words are useful for wayfinding and addressing purposes in malls, airports, sports arenas, libraries, and other public places, but it's quite common for my team and me to tour retail stores that use the least desirable words for communicating the best qualities of the brand. For instance, grocery stores regularly install giant letters with the words "DELI" and "PRODUCE" over their respective departments, which are not very appetizing. First of all, when's the last time you heard mom and dad telling their kids to "Eat your produce!"? If it must be words, we suggest "Fruits and Vegetables" as it's much more enticing and relatable to how consumers live. Secondly, there's a perceptual difference between a "delicatessen" and a "deli." A delicatessen conjures up images of an old-world neighborhood market that sells a selection of fine, exotic, or foreign prepared foods—henceforth *delicacies*. But your typical "deli" department in a grocery store is a place where a PTA parent with a hairnet, or an after-school teen, struggles to prepare, much less define what makes, a great-tasting pastrami and rye sandwich. Right or wrong, the perception consumers have is that the person who works in a delicatessen is an expert connoisseur of meat, bread, cheese, and toppings whereas the person who works at a deli is a worker counting the minutes until they can clock out. A "deli department" and a "delicatessen" suggest two different brand realms, and the choice of words matters because it sets the frame through which employees and customers will view the place.

Where stores get way off track, though, is when they try to communicate their unique brand values and intangible qualities—such as "family," "community," "heritage," "local," and "service"—through the use of literal words. Many years ago, I worked with an international grocery store chain that installed a massive sign that used the industry term "home-meal replacement" over the prepared foods department. The president asked me what I thought of this new program. My response: "Why don't you put 'bad parent' above the section?"

But if words aren't the answer, what is?

In the creative fields of writing and filmmaking, there's an often-repeated lesson that says, "Show, don't tell." In other words, don't *tell* readers or movie-goers what to *feel*. Instead, get them to experience the moment as if it were happening to them so their own thoughts, feelings, and heartbeats are racing rather than some marketing manager's slick voice-over or slogan.

As attention architects, we use a similar refrain in our design process: "Feel, don't tell." We live by this mantra because customers in stores connect better with things they can feel and experience for themselves on a sensory and emotional level.

Despite the advice that says people love to be told stories, we believe they prefer to feel like they're part of the story and storytelling, perhaps even co-authors of the brand, which is evident with the younger generation's intense involvement in the values and beliefs of brands like The Honest Company, Seventh Generation, Method, Everlane, and Fenty. And when it comes to building communities around bonfire moments, we find the more we build bonfires *with* them, not *for* them, the greater the bonfire magic and convening power will be.

Rather than using words like "quality," "family," or "community," our task as experience designers is to make sure our target audience can taste, touch, see, hear, smell, and feel things like community and family viscerally.

But how can you touch a feeling like community?

An international restaurant brand like Le Pain Quotidien does it exceptionally well by placing a large wooden farmhouse table smack dab in the middle of their restaurants. This impossible-to-miss feature and cultural icon is both functional and symbolic of the values of the Belgium-based culinary concept. Although the name of the brand is hard to pronounce for many people in other countries, the difficulty of the name has become part of its brand story, mystique, and mythology as an acquired taste of Europe.

We designed a similar scenario for Freson Bros. Instead of continuing to use signs that *tell* people about deep family values and community involvement, we created a community dining table with a fireplace and comfortable chairs that inspire friends and families to sit down and break bread together inside a grocery store so they can experience the deep longing and sense of community every day. It's become a neighborhood destination for Sunday brunch and gathering after games. Newer locations have gone further with this idea by including a craft beer bar—including their own local brew. Watching this *activity* of community-making happen in real time is a prime example of *feeling* a store's unique difference, not *telling* customers about it with marketing taglines and promotional slogans.

Our experience has also taught us that customers will stop to notice, connect, and engage with *visual information blocks*—whether it's a sign or a merchandising fixture—that attracts the involuntary eyes because of the *visual harmony*, but it doesn't stop there. Once we've captured the customer's eyes, we then try to deepen the conversation by helping them see our client's problem-solving capabilities in an emotionally resonant and memorable way.

For instance, hanging an old, faded bar and shield eagle sign inside a Harley-Davidson dealership engenders a sense of reverence and loyalty for their most avid riders who have a fear of the loss of freedom and lack of solidarity in our world. We know this works because we observe droves of customers stopping to pay homage and take pictures in front of this iconic sign.

One of the institutionalized terms the retail and grocery industry uses is "decor" as a catchall word for the store's interior. But we find this term problematic as words are critical in setting the right frame and expectation for internal managers. The term "decor" implies the interior experience is about *decoration* when it's about visual processing, human comprehension, and brand coherency.

The simple act of banishing the word "decor" from the retail and grocery store lexicon does a lot to help retailers rethink the purpose of signage and the goal of the store experience. While on one level signage is there to provide an address for products, the more important goal is to signal and impart the brand's added value, standards of care, and detailed curation process they go through on behalf of customers.

4. PRODUCT VS. CONTEXT

Our elders tell us, "Don't judge a book by its cover." Though well-intentioned advice, it doesn't entirely reflect the primitive parts of our brains that have had to make snap judgments for thousands of years to survive and thrive in our habitats. We're hardwired to judge things by their covers because, in previous eras of lions, wolves, and marauding tribes, that's how our ancestors stayed alive.

As evolved as we might seem today, this split-second context scanning and decision-making process never left us. It's still a core part of our environmental awareness and innate survival system. While we're not conscious of it, we prefer the world around us to be stable and predictable because it gives us a sense of control over our environment. But deep down, we know stability isn't always possible. So no matter where we are, we're constantly on the lookout for contextual clues and the slightest changes in our environment.

Being in the restaurant-design industry for over thirty years, I learned long ago that patrons don't always notice the incredible effort and money we spend on grand sweeping gestures like columns, stairways, doors, and windows as much as they do the little details. Whether walking into a bar, café, or high-end steak house, customers scan the environment to assess everything from the chairs and server uniforms all the way down to the plateware, tablecloths, and salt and pepper shakers to extract vital information about the restaurant's quality, caliber, and expertise. Without being aware of it, they make all kinds of snap judgments about these details. Get these signals wrong, and it doesn't matter how great the architecture, food, or service is or where the chef trained in France.

All great restaurant operators and chefs will tell you that presentation is everything in the food business. But it doesn't come cheap, nor without effort. If anything, it's intentionally *effortful* by design. The amount of time, energy, and creative focus restaurants expend to "plate up" their food in appetizing, tempting, and photo-worthy ways is substantial. Successful bars and restaurants understand this contextual art of "plating up" food so well that they make it a standard part of their training and daily operation. The best operators know that "plating up" their tables matters too. Something as simple as flowers on the table or in the restrooms can dramatically change the perception and rating of a restaurant's quality. Customers will overlook or forgive other concerning factors because of this extra little touch.

While the average customer takes it for granted, the cost of purchasing, washing, maintaining, and dealing with glassware breakage is a sizable line item on the spreadsheet for restaurant expenses. But no matter how much more efficient and durable it might be, there's a reason they don't serve martinis in coffee cups. The delicate martini glass is a core part of the purchase experience of eating out, making patrons feel special, like they received a gift with the sensual olive and toothpick added in for a twist.

Yet far too many retailers ignore the critical role that context and presentation play in attracting consumers, influencing their behavior, and shaping their perceptions. Some retail operators complain it takes too much time and additional work to "plate" their products up in seductive ways. But overlooking the importance of context makes the products unappetizing and undifferentiated, prompting customers to view them as mere price-driven commodities.

Whether we're working on a restaurant or a retail store, our goal, metaphorically speaking, is to make the product "taste great" before our customers have even taken a bite out of it. Most of the companies we work for make excellent products. Their problem, however, is that they don't get credit for their hard work due to the lack of context and presentation.

Context is king in terms of influencing consumer behavior and perception management. Therefore, we don't believe in ever leaving the literal product on a plate or shelf to defend itself on its own. Like supporting a talented actor onstage, we know that to win the customer's interest and engagement, we must surround the product with the right context, costumes, props, and supporting elements to "set the scene" and get the brand story to stick unconsciously in the audience's gut.

In the mid-2000s, Nabisco, the 125-year-old manufacturer of cookies and snacks, hired our firm to help them address a concerning trend: less than 45 percent of customers in the average grocery store were going down the cookie and cracker aisle where their iconic products—OREO cookies, Chips Ahoy!, Triscuit crackers, Nilla Wafers, and other legacy brands—sat increasingly underutilized. Like most of the assignments we get, we couldn't change the product, price, packaging, or ingredient mixes. But we could change the context.

During our discovery phase, we learned that fewer customers were venturing into the cookie and cracker aisle because of the negative publicity around ingredients such as trans-fatty acids. While our client had adjusted their ingredient mix long ago, the unhealthy perception stuck to the aisle. Instead of relying on the zany, cartoony packaging to make the sale—which we believed made the perception worse—we created an in-store brand realm called "Mom's Kitchen" and surrounded the products with the contextual cues of cookie jars, rolling pins, flour, and a symbolic kitchen table, which evoked nostalgic memories. (Think Martha Stewart and Norman Rockwell planning a picnic basket or bag lunch for you and your family with cookies, crackers, cheese, sliced meats, and jams, and you'll get the picture of our design concept.) We didn't come up with these ideas randomly or out of thin air. Instead, we uncovered these powerful artifacts and portals of meaning by observing customers in their homes and seeing how they use, store, and think about cookies and crackers in their daily lives.

This breakthrough concept was radical at the time because we dared propose removing standard inventory aisles and creating perceptual rooms. Customers embraced Mom's Kitchen wholeheartedly, increasing sales by 18 to 36 percent in half a dozen test-store sites while boosting customer engagement, dwell times, and product experimentation, which social scientist Paco Underhill of the research firm Envirosell helped us verify. By shifting the brand's image from peddling unhealthy products to more of the wholesome family tradition, we helped our client get more credit for what they did well.

Getting a place's context right requires a deep interest, broad knowledge, and sincere curiosity in the cultural signs, symbols, and meanings around the globe, throughout history, and within pop culture. It also demands being a student of culture without judgment, condescension, or cynicism and respecting the multitudes of cultural meanings out there. Therefore, our firm has developed an extensive library of cultural symbols and robust catalogs of icons and artifacts that are part of the universal language of meaning and communication. We make it a daily practice to hunt for and share the cultural symbols we've uncovered with our teammates. But we don't ever glom these cultural meanings onto a client's place or brand if it doesn't genuinely fit who they are because consumers will spot this inauthenticity a mile away. Instead, we have to ensure our clients can claim these cultural meanings with some level of credibility, authority, and expertise. And if you get it right—no slick marketing or copywriter words are needed.

5. WALKING VS. MILLING

Many retailers we work with justify their store's extra-wide aisles because, according to surveys, their customers say they want them. This rationale may make logical sense. But when customers shop fast, they engage less with the product offerings and ultimately buy less. And when they shop quickly, they tend to treat the store in a more transactional fashion.

Whether designing a grocery store, home improvement store, or even orchestra, we spend a lot of time observing whether people walk with haste, eyes forward, and determination to get in and out of the venue as quickly as possible or with a sense of exploration, discovery, milling around, and meandering behavior. The latter "window shopping" behavior means we're doing our jobs right of keeping the customer engaged; the former means we have much more work to do to improve customer engagement and stave off online alternatives. (We dive deeper into these behaviors in chapter seven, where you'll find a detailed list of fundamental questions to help uncover these buried insights.)

Studying how customers enter a place and how they leave provides far more valuable information than most designers or operators realize. If customers look beat down, haggard, and tired on their way out, we know something about the experience is wearing them down, and we need to find the source of that "energy drain" and fix it. But if they walk out excited, talking about their experience with smiles, and enthused by what they saw, we know we're on the right path to filling their tanks with energy.

Old-world merchants intuitively understood the importance of customers' walking speed, eye focus, and body language. They knew that to get people to linger, browse, and mill around, they'd have to do something to catch their attention, slow them down, and reward them with pleasure. As a result, they did everything they could—from creating fabulous seafood displays to offering free coffee and apple cider—to get potential customers to look, stop, browse, and chat for a bit. But the layout of many retail stores today resembles that of a hyper-efficient warehouse or lumberyard of inventoried products for the convenience of forklifts, not humans. These "expressway aisles" only encourage fast walking, lower levels of product engagement, and a commodity mindset, opening the door to faster, easier alternatives.

As ambitious as it sounds, we want customers to view the store as a place of leisure, recreation, and enjoyment, not a place of work, chores, and commodity transactions. When customers walk into the store in a rushed and deliberate manner and never slow down, rather than a curious, explorative, and mean-dering zigzag pattern, we know the store needs to work on engagement. While surveys say customers "just want to get in and out," our job as place-makers and place-operators is to divide their initial intentions by making the place so enjoyable and the experience so rewarding that they want to stay for a while and come back more often. If they're milling around the store engaged, we know we're on the right path to long-term success.

6. INFORMATION OVERLOAD VS. SENSORY DEPRIVATION

Humans have always preferred the beautiful over the unattractive and the stim-ulating over the monotonous. On a basic level, our definitions of beauty and unattractiveness haven't changed that much throughout history or cultures. Universally we still prefer qualities like symmetry, composition, rhythm, scale, repetition, proportion, contrast, and surprise. It would take another book to explain why humans seek beautiful things. But the short answer is that, histor-ically, the things we found attractive to our senses had survival value, whereas we avoided things that could harm us or threaten our existence.

Unfortunately, many venues such as the grocery store aisle, DMV, or post office often don't qualify as places humans consider attractive, inviting, or stimulating. If anything, people are turned off and dread going to them, which is problematic for places in today's digital alternative world. But places don't need to be "prettified" or "intellectualized." Instead, they need to be intuitively "experiential" and tap into our senses in a way that attracts our attention and makes us want to be there.

On any given day, we experience a wide range of environments that produce different types of sensations, feelings, emotions, and perceptions within us. One of the major factors in determining how we feel in a space is the quality and quantity of sensory stimuli we encounter, which act to either arouse or annoy us.

The term "information overload" is tossed around casually, but it's a real biological state of feeling mentally and physically overwhelmed. We all know this feeling of being tapped out if we've spent a day shopping for furniture or traversing a hot, sticky, crowded theme park full of signs, lines, and competing requests for our attention. Even if the products and experiences are well designed, too much stimulation (good or bad) can push us over the edge and reduce our ability to engage with our environment.

This same feeling also happens at industry conferences and trade shows. While we might hear impressive speakers or tour fascinating booths, the longer we stay inside a large, windowless, scaleless building with a surplus of products, promotions, people, sounds, smells, and colors screaming for our attention, the more our ability to comprehend and retain the information diminishes. We can usually restore our body's energy and refresh our minds by simply going outside, breathing fresh air, and seeing blue skies. This observation explains why so many conference-goers rush outside on their breaks to get some fresh air before having to head back into brain-drain mode.

But why does nature restore and refresh our minds so well?

My team and I argue nature has a natural math to it that feels both resolved and mysteriously enchanting. Something as simple as a blue sky, a field of grass, grove of trees, or even the inside of an orange can captivate our interest and fill our tanks with energy. My team and I bring the same organic principles of nature's visual enchantment inside stores as much as we can while balancing the needs of function and order. While there are hundreds of design variables to play with, we find using these six variables—hierarchy, order, structure, rhythm, scale, and contrast—helps us the most, just as they do in music.

While information overload is typically our top concern for not draining people's batteries, the opposite state—*sensory deprivation*—also needs to be considered and avoided. Many government buildings, such as courthouses, social services, and other institutional facilities, can be so cold, monotonous, and uninspiring that they rob us of our energy and lead to impatience and irritability. The same is true of many schools and classrooms where students struggle to pay attention for long periods. Some office buildings, shopping centers, hospitals, and housing projects also struggle to captivate our attention because of the uniformity, blandness, and homogeneity of their environments.

The key to attention and engagement is finding that sweet spot between information overload and sensory deprivation where the public feels interested and engaged by the place but not overwhelmed. My team and I spend a lot of time inside the projects we design to see whether the occupants are having a good or bad time, when and where they're socializing and bonding with others, and when and where they're antisocial and unfriendly to others. Of course, we closely study the metrics of the number of daily visits and length of time spent at the venues, particularly compared to other options in the market. One of the great benefits of working in retail is it allows us to measure increases in sales velocity, dwell times, and product experimentation by studying how consumers behave and make purchase decisions within inches of the products. Not only does this measurable information help us improve the performance of these retail venues, but it also helps keep the public engaged in other non-commercial projects such as live performance venues, universities, and urban districts.

DO LESS, BETTER

When I entered design school in 1983, I was "visually illiterate," as most newbie designers are. But after thirty-five years of learning how to see, practicing my craft, testing design ideas in the field, and studying the results, my team and I have become masters at attracting people's attention and getting them engaged enthusiastically in their environment without them consciously realizing it. And it's a lot of fun teaching clients these skills as it allows them to quickly see the world through a new lens while improving sales and consumer loyalty.

However, most business and institutional leaders don't have thirty-five years to learn a challenging new skill like architectural design, graphic communication, and environmental psychology. But once we arm them with the basic design ingredients for visually attracting people's attention and improving the engagement of a space, they can begin to effectively see, assess, and improve their spaces on their own.

While there are thousands of variables to play with in design, if I had to summarize what makes a place perfect, it is usually a function of not adding anything to the design that is extraneous, unnecessary, or requires too much mental or physical work. Striking this experiential chord is extremely difficult. The secret lies not in adding more things into the design concept but instead taking items out. Much like in music, film, and art, editing out the superfluous stuff is the true gift of someone who knows their craft. When evaluating why a space or scene isn't working, my team and I will keep pulling stuff out until we reach an overall state of *visual harmony*. With this absence of visual noise, we stand a much better chance of getting customers emotionally engaged, which we'll discuss in the next chapter.

The Emotional Quotient of Place

"We do ourselves a disservice when we think of human beings as exclusively logic- or knowledge-driven, and fail to pay attention to the role of the emotions. The two systems are enmeshed because that is the way our brain and our organism have been put together by evolution."

—Antonio R. Damasio

"COME ON, NINA! THAT'S RIDICULOUS!" my dad said to my mom, more agitated than I thought he should've been about such a small matter. "There are NO NEW COLORS! That'd be like saying there are new temperatures!"

"What do you mean there aren't any new colors, Cecil?!" my mom snapped back. "There are new colors coming out every year! I just read that this year's new color is mauve!"

"Did you just say *mauve* with a slight French accent?" My dad snickered. "Mauve isn't a new color. That's just what some designer in SoHo puts in your head so you'll keep buying new pillows, bedsheets, and towels every year to replace the perfectly good ones you already have!"

While I had my mom's back, I had to admit Dad had a point. From a purely technical perspective, there aren't any new colors. Colors, like many things we process via our senses, are subjective. But I understood my mom's attraction to fashion and her knack for keeping up with the ever-changing trends.

As an eight-year-old kid sitting in the back seat of my dad's 1970s Caprice Classic on the way to Sears for the annual linen sale, I could see the differences in my parents' DNA on full display. It was oddly terrifying yet incredibly instructional. Listening to their debates gave me a healthy balance of reason and emotion, logic and passion, and facts and feelings. It also taught me volumes about how two people could see the same situation differently and how I could address competing agendas as a future architect and strategic advisor to clients.

EASIER VERSUS BETTER (A.K.A. THE CECIL VERSUS NINA CHRONICLES)

My dad is pragmatic and has no patience for the "touchy-feely-fluffy" stuff, as he likes to call it. He's worked hard all his life to buy a home and fill it up once with sturdy furniture and never get rid of it. But his practicality can sometimes land him in the doghouse. For instance, he once tried to put all the power outlets above the couch because he argued it'd make plugging things in easier. That domestic crisis entailed my parents calling me late one night to have a mediation session about whether there was an official standard on what height electrical outlets must be in a house. There is. My dad lost that argument, but not before leaving a mangled series of holes across the living room wall. If my mom wasn't around and Dad had his way, he'd paint the entire house one color to save money and put floor drains in the middle of each room to make hosing them down easier.

My mother, by stark contrast, likes things more sensual and imaginative. She likes to spend her hard-earned dollars coming up with creative ways to change things up in our family home. She puts incredible thought and effort into decorating each room with a distinctive paint color, wallpaper treatment, furniture period, and studied adornments that perfectly fit into a sub-theme my father struggles to follow. Like many of the other Ninas, she views her home, and the carefully curated contents placed within it, as biographical expressions of our family's values and identity and tangible reminders of our hopes, dreams, and aspirations.

When it comes to shopping in stores, my father and mother couldn't be more opposite. Cecil enters most stores with the mindset that it's a *Hunger Games*-style competition—a time-trial obstacle course of sorts—that he has to complete as quickly and efficiently as possible to claim victory. When Nina, however, visits one of her favorite stores—say Costco, Williams Sonoma, or Nordstrom—all she sees are possibilities for how she can nurture, enrich, and enhance her family's life. While Nina enjoys taking her time to stroll around the aisles and explore the future scenarios of how this item might go well with that one, Cecil becomes an impatient driver, mowing people down with his shopping cart and whizzing by half the items he needs to get on our family's shopping list.

The differences between Nina's and Cecil's viewpoints beg the question of the purpose of places. Is home just a place to sleep, eat, and "hold a roof over your head," as my dad declares, or is it the "nest" where you nurture your family and make your dreams come true? Is a restaurant just a place to refuel your body's tank, or is it a place to relax, indulge in conversation, and have an experience? Is an office just a place to warehouse employees, or is it a base camp for passionate believers to unite around a shared mission and hash out strategic plans for changing the world? And is a store just a warehouse to stack inventory and transact sales, or is it a resource center for solving problems, finding great ideas for living better, and fulfilling your dreams?

In practice, my mom and dad are both emotional shoppers, as we all are. But my dad sees shopping as a race, whereas my mom sees it as a leisurely stroll around the park. Many business-minded managers often dismiss emotions as the "fluffy" nonbusiness stuff, but they do so at their peril because to be human is to be emotional. As the brilliant author and neuroscientist Antonio R. Damasio described in his outstanding book *Descartes' Error: Emotion, Reason, and the Human Brain*, "Emotions and feelings are not a luxury; they are a means of communicating our states of mind to others. But they are also a way of guiding our own judgments and decisions. Emotions bring the body into the loop of reason."

IT'S TIME TO SHIFT THE BALANCE

Having spent my life mediating between Nina and Cecil as well as in a career studying the impact places have on our physical, emotional, and social well-being, I recognize the importance of having a home and store that are about both function and dreams, organization and inspiration, and utility and expression. But far too many retail organizations I encounter have a lopsided management approach where they skew mostly toward supply-side thinkers and ultra-pragmatists (the Cecils) but don't have enough creative and imaginative thinkers (the Ninas) at the strategy table. The Ninas are the "situation creators" who instinctively know how to draw people into stores and create desire and demand for their unique experience value proposition. They also understand how to appeal to customers' senses and make them feel confident, secure, and empowered to pursue their dreams while shopping.

Don't get me wrong; I'm sensitive to maintenance and cost issues of managing stores and the operational as well as logistical challenges of loading them up daily with products. But when the store experience becomes boring, monotonous, and homogeneous for customers, it can make visiting them a physical drag and mental drain. While the utilitarian approach to retail prevailed for many decades during the era when there was more customer demand than supply of retail stores, it typically came at the cost of customers' ability to enjoy their shopping experience. But now that Nina, and other customers like her, have many more options for where, when, and how to shop, operating uninspiring, emotionless stores is coming at the loss of sales, frequency of visits, and loyalty for many old-school retailers.

Though I've called them "Cecils" and "Ninas," this rational versus emotional mindset is not gender-specific or even gender-related. I encounter female Cecils and male Ninas everywhere I go, from the consumers I observe in the field to the management leaders I work with in boardrooms. I've listened closely to the debates between the uber-efficient leaders and the emotion-evoking visual storytellers. They both make excellent points but must be aware of the times we're living in and strike the right balance. And right now, the utilitarian warehouse approach to retail isn't working out as well for brick-and-mortar stores because of the incredible utility and ruthless efficiency of the internet. So instead of focusing all their energies on the "transactional buying side," retailers need to intensify their "relational/shopping demand side."

As surprising as this may sound, many retail leaders I meet don't like to shop. But if you're going to be in the retail business today, you not only have to keep up with the trends; you have to try to lead them. You also must understand the powerful role emotions play in influencing consumer behavior in the store. And, of course, you must have some passion for the joy of shopping. If not, you're in the wrong business.

The most innovative retailers know how to arouse our senses, tap into our emotions, and channel this combined human energy down a choreographed path—just like a gripping movie or live theater does as part of the unfolding journey of their show, which we'll dive into in chapter six, "The Theater of Place." By carefully crafting each scene with strategically placed stimuli, these directors of the eye know how to arrest our attention and keep us glued to their content, leading to much higher consumer engagement and performance throughout every inch of the store.

While some might accuse these innovative store designers of manipulating consumers, customers want to have fun and enjoy their shopping experience. They don't want to feel like they have to do an exhausting chore or endure mental calculus. Instead, they want to get turned on to new ideas and products that can enhance the quality of their lives and be entertained and enlightened by an irresistible brand story and quest while tending to daily tasks.

Instead of leaving the store experience to chance, retailers can play an active role in shaping the direction of their customers' emotions by crafting captivating scenes and dramatic moments that elicit specific customer feelings and transport them from a rational, conscious state of mind into a realm of imagination, reflection, and possibility.

But how do you identify those emotions? By starting with your customer's "Dream of Someday," which everyone has, including Cecil.

THE DREAM OF SOMEDAY

After thirty-five years of watching customers shop, I can usually predict the specific task they need to "get done," such as picking up milk or diapers, just by reading their faces and observing their body language. But that's just one of the many things they have on their minds. That same customer also carries around a right pocket full of hopes, dreams, and aspirations and a left pocket full of fears, failures, and frustrations while they shop. What goes on inside the customer's mind while shopping is analogous to driving a car or walking to work. When doing those activities, we don't need to focus 100 percent of our mental faculties on driving or walking because our subconscious brains and sensory systems make many decisions for us. Instead, we have a cascade of thoughts, ideas, and ruminations swirling in our minds. Customers bring this same multitude of thoughts with them into the store while shopping.

Retailers can transform their stores from chores to more by framing them as a place to help customers solve problems and indulge in their "Dream of Someday." For some customers, that Dream of Someday might be losing five pounds through an easy-but-flavorful Mediterranean diet plan, and for others, it might be planning the perfect Thanksgiving meal for a big extended family get-together. For some, it might be building the dream closet organizing system, and for others, a wood deck off the back of their house with a fancy BBQ grill, sound system, and hot tub.

The point is: we all have dreams—you, me, Nina, and, yes, even Cecil. But sometimes we have to dig around to find them or take the people we care about to the right place to witness these yearnings seep out. Part of a retailer's job is to identify customers' dreams and find creative ways for the store experience to bring these aspirations to life. But far too many stores prevent customers from dreaming because they're hyper-rational, hard to shop in, and don't allow customers to enter an imaginary realm or consumer fantasy. Instead, they remind the customers they're running late, wasting time, not having fun, and losing money. Or worse, they put them in a defensive posture by approaching them too quickly or aggressively as they prioritize "hitting this quarter's numbers," then appealing to the customers' emotions.

Admittedly, my team and I are obsessed, if not neurotic, about how customers perceive and behave when confronted with our clients' sales teams and environments. We pay close attention to the setup and processes of the sales situations to zero in on which aspects of their layout, approach, and experience are turning customers off and sparking undesirable emotions and which are allowing customers to enter their ideal Dream of Someday state.

THE TYPICAL CAR-BUYING EXPERIENCE

Buying a vehicle is one of the most dreaded purchasing experiences consumers have to endure. While price, features, maintenance packages, financing, and vehicle options are already stressful enough to make sense of, consumers dread getting the runaround from sly and cunning salespeople.

Car salesmen (emphasis on men here) make the situation worse with subtle details. They wear starched-white shirts (power broker) tucked in neat and tight and fitted out to the nines with signals of success (fancy watches, jewelry, belts), making them look like masters in control of their domain. They position their desks, phones, pens, staplers, computer monitors, and high-back chairs in a commanding perch to overlook the sales floor (shark tank), so they can see which customers (prey) walk onto the sales floor (trap) and show interest (take the bait) for a potential product.

When customers sit down with salespeople, their chairs are often smaller and less comfortable, and their backs face the crowd, triggering primal instincts about being approached or attacked from behind. They have no familiarity with what all the numbers mean on the screen, nor do they have an in-depth understanding of which financial options are wisest for them to pursue. Worst of all, they must reveal their naked financial history to a complete stranger.

This vulture/prey dynamic makes customers feel emotionally inferior, weak, and diminutive, which destroys the opportunity of getting them into the Dream of Someday mindset.

Everything about this typical car sale scenario feels off-putting for customers and triggers the most primal emotions humans have: the fear of losing control and being put in a vulnerable position. My team and I try to remove any semblance of the "shark tank" feeling and cues that signal to "watch your back!" Instead of the typical power desk with high-back chairs aiming toward smaller customer chairs, we place round, unassigned coffee shop–style tables with non-assigned and non-hierarchical chairs that put customers at ease and make them feel like they're on equal footing with the salespeople. Unlike showrooms of the past, we try to make customers feel empowered, confident, and in charge of their decision-making, not vulnerable and weak as so frequently happens.

Most customers we've interviewed prefer to see, touch, feel, smell, drive, and experience the cars and options in person. However, many are heading online because it allows them to avoid the psychological discomfort of confronting and playing poker with an aggressive, steely-eyed car salesperson who is much better at the high-stakes match than they are. But it's not just car dealerships that embody this stressful customer/sales dynamic; so do many other places of commerce.

THE TYPICAL FURNITURE STORE EXPERIENCE

Traditionally, many furniture stores locate their shops in commercial corridors or near the mall in big-box stores and outparcel sites. Inside these voluminous stores are hundreds of little vignettes of couches, dining room tables, chairs, credenzas, bedroom sets, and leather and upholstery samples.

While well intended and rational, the first problem with this big-box approach is asking consumers to proactively come into the store to make a big-ticket purchase. The second problem lies in how overwhelming these environments are to our senses and emotions.

Lifestyle brands like Crate & Barrel let go of the big-box store approach to squeeze themselves into the tighter confines of outdoor shopping centers and main streets where there are a variety of other activities happening, such as eating out at restaurants, seeing movies, and hanging out with a leisurely "walk-around-the-park" mind state. This less deliberate sales approach allows customers to casually enter the store in "just browsing" mode, while encouraging "milling" behavior, which has a surprisingly high success rate of inspiring customers to redecorate their homes. Even Cecil gets spontaneously inspired from time to time as he stumbles upon a great idea, like a waffle maker, coffee grinder, or cocktail shaker.

This approach works well because it reduces the anxiety, stress, and worry of a more deliberate approach and allows customers the mental space and frame of mind to imagine and enter these ideal dream-state scenarios naturally and casually. When customers make these discoveries on their own, it allows them to feel more spontaneously inspired, empowered, and in control. It's not uncommon for my team and me to see customers walk out of the store with an entirely unintended purchase: a new dining room table or bedroom set. It happens more often than you may realize.

While we may pick up milk and bread from the grocery store every week, most of us don't visit traditional furniture stores to buy big, bulky, expensive furniture that often. It's a once-every-three-to-eight-years kind of thing (or never for Cecil). So you don't have a lot of accidental purchases taking place in these establishments because they require a deliberate and premeditated trip.

The low foot traffic in furniture stores can make salespeople feel hungry for a sale and starving for customer contact. Yet, many furniture stores exacerbate this dynamic of customer anxiety by positioning their sales counters smack-dab in the front of the store. We've all seen that ravenous look in the eye of a desperate car salesperson approaching us as soon as we pull into the parking lot, and it's not all that different in some furniture stores. It's an uncomfortable situation for a customer to be put in and triggers an immediate defensive posture instead of allowing them to dream about what a new purchase might do for them.

Many years of studying store behavior taught us that customers dread these high-pressure, defensive selling environments. Furniture stores are already overwhelming enough to wrap one's head around from a sensory level, much less to be bothered by an overly aggressive salesperson. While some furniture brands don't deploy these tactics, plenty of other aggressive brands do, which soured the punch for the industry and left a bad taste in customers' mouths. Giving customers room to dream by themselves and imagine the possibilities for how their homes can be improved and transformed by acquiring the right piece of furniture should be the store operators' primary objective.

THE DREADED "HOME SALES CENTER" APPROACH

Buying furniture or a new car is a sizable purchase to consider. But they don't compare to the stress, anxiety, and financial proctology involved in finding a new home, negotiating prices, qualifying for a mortgage, and figuring out how to come up with the hefty down payment. Nor do they compare to the emotional hurdles and psychological apprehensions that some people—particularly older generations—have for uprooting themselves to move from one place to another.

The Dream of Someday mindset can be a fun state of mind to be in, but customers' stress levels can ratchet up significantly when considering the exact steps and requirements of changing where they reside, who they live next door to, and how they can afford to finance a new place. And when customers are worried and anxious, they can shut down their imaginations and become very irritable, defensive, and prickly. For those selling homes, the job should be to help customers get comfortable and inspired by the benefits of change. The goal should be to prevent these anxiety-ridden concerns and stress-inducing chemicals from flooding customers so they can dream and imagine the possibilities for how much better their lives might be in the future by moving to a new place.

Yet, what do most housing developments do to reduce this stress? They call their first point of customer contact the "sales center," which, for prospective customers, translates to entering a shark tank with hungry, aggressive predators waiting for their next meal tickets to arrive.

For the work we do in the home building industry, we ask that they strike the words "salespeople," "sales call," and "sales center" from their lexicon. Instead of the cliché and dreaded sales center format, we create community coffee shops and wine bars where staff can invite visitors for a drink to learn about the power of community, neighborhoods, and life-improvement opportunities in their housing development. We go to great lengths to make these places not just for potential customers but for community residents as well. Why? So potential customers can see evidence and social proof of people similar to them who made the same major life change and successfully transitioned to a new place.

We create self-discovery zones and self-guided tours where potential home-buyers can see examples and testimonials of real customers talking about how a change of residence improved their lives. And we let them dream and imagine their new lives for a while before having a staff member approach them.

RETAIL AS DREAM THERAPY

Whenever I visit my family in the South, my dad and I often take a drive to Bass Pro Shops, the local Tractor Supply store, or Topgolf's reinvention of the traditional driving range into a social gathering place. While there's no specific item we need to pick up, my father finds these retail field trips therapeutic and conducive to talking about life, family, and the future; and I enjoy witnessing these rare emotional moments during these Dream of Someday field trips.

As we walk and talk our way through the store, he'll tell me about his dream of someday buying a fishing boat and moving to river country, getting a new set of irons and taking his golf game up a few notches, or purchasing a riding mower complete with a radio, headlights, and cup holders that'd be overkill for his small patch of grass. Despite rarely coming home with a new boat or riding mower, we almost always buy something, such as fishing poles and putters. These purchases are a small price to pay to get to hang out with him as he talks about his hopes and dreams, while reminding me of how much retail stores spark emotionally rich conversations.

Whether you sell riding mowers to Cecil, mauve linens to Nina, or flaming red Harley motorcycles to Ernie, the aim of your place should be to help your target customers enter and stay in their Dream of Someday state from the beginning to the end of the store experience. That not only helps attract customers to your venue regularly, but it also helps deepen their interest and engagement in your offering as well as your brand.

Nina and Cecil are still arguing over color trends, furniture styles, and the need for new towels, which to me is what makes them so endearing. The good news is that the retail world is big enough to have plenty of great options for the two of them to dream and find what they're looking for. My dad can go to Lowe's and Bass Pro Shops to have his moments fetishizing over lawn mowers and fishing equipment, and my mom can shop at Williams Sonoma and Kiehl's to discover new products and remedies she's never experimented with before. My dad will continue thinking of shopping primarily as a conquest and procurement task, and my mom will view shopping as recreation, leisure, and inspiration. I'm good with both viewpoints as they each have their place in the rational/emotional consumer's mind.

Where I get frustrated, though, is the binary debate I see in business, boardrooms, and books declaring that the ruthless efficiency of Amazon or Shopify has finally won out over the romance of life and that retail is dead. Retail is not dead, but utilitarian retail is dead because there's now a much faster, cheaper, and more convenient way to acquire cheap commodities online if that's all you're looking to purchase. Human beings, however, want more than commodities and have desires greater than their possessions.

The debates between function versus emotion, literal versus imaginative, and rock-bottom prices versus high-fidelity curation have been going on for generations in retail and will continue long into the future. Fortunately, there's enough room in the market for many players and positions to win. However, the critical difference today is the more extreme positions—like 99 Cents Only Stores and Whole Foods, Marshalls and Chanel, Petco and Pagerie—stick deeper in the minds of consumers than mushy middle-of-the-road generalist concepts like department stores that came of age when there was more supply than demand for retail options.

If your organization is more like Cecil and refuses to change or adjust to a new world reality, I suggest you dispense with the cost of building, running, and maintaining stores and go online to join the commodity game. But it's important to know up front that the barriers to entry online are much lower, the focus on price is higher, and the customer acquisition costs are staggering.

If your organization is more like Nina in that you want to keep up with, or better yet, lead the fashion of the times, then focus on creating memorable experiences that can tap into emotions, fulfill dreams, and bring tears of joy to your customers' eyes.

The "Form and Shape" of Place

*"Humans, like all other animals, are selective crea-
tures; that is, our survival and flourishing depend on
our ongoing, mostly unconscious, selection of aspects
of our environment for attention, interaction, and
transformation. So, objects are events with meanings
that 'stand out' within the context of a situation."*
**—Mark Johnson, *The Aesthetics of
Meaning and Thought***

GROWING UP IN THE SOUTH, I thought a mandolin was an instrument you
played in a bluegrass band, and the only Julienne I'd ever known was our high
school's French teacher. But many years later, while waiting for my wife to buy
a gift at a fancy cooking store, I saw a sign that said, "50% off on mandolines—
The best way to julienne vegetables!"

"Huh?" I thought. "Why would French chefs use a musical instrument to cook vegetables?"

After a few minutes of trying to solve the complex riddle of *What in the world does this weird-looking contraption do?* I gave up and moved on to the next shiny object that caught my eye: a multideck gas grill! My caveman's brain knew exactly what I could do with that! Images of backyard BBQs with the boys watching Sunday football and having a few brewskies, burgers, and bratwurst by the pool flashed before my eyes.

A few months later, though, I was watching a celebrity chef on TV, and wouldn't you know, he broke out a mandoline and described it as the most valuable tool in his kitchen. After seeing him slice and dice vegetables with not only ease but grace, I was hooked! I bought one the next day, while telling everyone I knew about how life-changing mandolines are.

This fascinating eureka moment—when consumers finally get the value of what something new and initially unidentifiable can do for them—is a pivotal turning point for those involved in retail, design, and business model reinvention to better understand how consumer behavior works in their field.

"SO WHAT CAN I DO WITH THAT THING?"

Think back to the first time you saw a two-wheeled, self-balancing personal transporter Segway or heard about people paying $35–70 to ride a stationary bike at Soul Cycle for forty-five minutes while an instructor yells self-help advice at you. Whenever we encounter something new and unfamiliar, whether an object, building, or cultural trend, we can't help but ask ourselves, "What can I do with that?" It's usually not a question we ask out loud but something that happens underneath the radar of our consciousness as a natural part of our brain's automatic environmental scanning, sorting, and filtering system.

As described in chapter three, this processing starts with a combination of our memories and senses. Like a reconnaissance team, our eyes and other senses constantly scan our environment for two critical things: *enhancements* or *impediments* to life. But this sense-making capacity requires lots of energy, most of which is fueled in the human body by a form of sugar called glucose, and because the brain is so rich in nerve cells, or neurons, it's the most energy-demanding organ we have, using over one-half of all the sugar energy in the body. Solving this problem of limited brain power requires our more energy-efficient subconscious system to take over the bulk of our decision-making and work in the background to conserve energy by doing predictive coding.

There are many different definitions and debates about predictive coding. But our team defines it as an automatic process our brain uses to quickly scan our environment and make microsecond decisions regarding two critical questions: "What is this thing?" and "How can it help or hurt me?" We rely on this predictive coding mechanism because it reduces our need to study everything around us in exhausting detail. Instead, our background thinking assesses the "form and shape" of things in front of us quickly to see if they match something we already know and are familiar with, such as a BBQ grill. But sometimes, we don't know what something is—say, a chef-grade mandoline—which alerts the conscious brain to get involved or dismiss it as inconsequential.

Why is this sense-making capacity important to the business of places?

THE PREDICTABLE "FORMS AND SHAPES" OF THE BUILT WORLD

You could take the signs off most malls, drugstores, gas stations, convenience stores, grocery stores, department stores, fast-food joints, and car dealerships, and the public would still be able to identify the use of these buildings. This instant typological recognition of these places' standard form and shape is because people have ingrained memories of them from past experiences. Therefore, our conscious brains don't need to pay too much attention to them to know what they are for and what we can do with them, which is not always a good thing.

For instance, when we see a building that looks like a gas station or a convenience store, we don't have to overthink what we can do there or what the experience will be like. Our preconditioned brains know we can fill up our car with gas and run in to grab a soda, beer, gum, or a pack of smokes. We typically don't expect to get handmade sushi, fresh organic vegetables, or the best cuts of meat inside a gas station or convenience store, even though consumers would love to find these kinds of higher quality product offerings in a small corner store format.

The convenience store has traditionally appealed to a narrow audience heavily focused on men, construction workers, technicians, teens, and loiterers who feel comfortable there. But many women, kids, professionals, hipsters, and the fashion-forward crowd don't feel as comfortable, representing a lot of money left on the table.

The common assumption by many consumers is that traditional convenience stores and gas stations don't have something for them or are not places designed for their needs or identity. This perception explains why these industries have struggled to evolve with society and move beyond just selling gas, sodas, beer, and cigarettes. Not unlike an actor who is known for one type of film, these ubiquitous concepts are stuck in a typecast role in what some experts consider a dying retail genre. This inability to shift the consumer's mind to other product categories has executives and investors at convenience stores nervous about the future.

To make matters worse, many in the convenience store industry believe these top-selling items—sugary snacks, sodas, gas, cigarettes, and tobacco products—are all under attack by food activists, concerned parents, and government regulators, and many of them might not be around as much in the future. Even though Elon Musk and Tesla dominate the conversation, most car companies, including Cadillac, Chrysler, BMW, Mini, Jaguar, and Bentley, have already committed to reinventing themselves as EV-only brands, which, of course, means no gas and no need to stop at the gas station anymore. These industries will have to do something as California has approved rules to ban the sale of new gasoline-powered cars by 2035, and cities and towns across the state are already banning gas stations as one of many measures to combat climate change in a region devastated by wildfires and drought. And what happens in the Golden State eventually spreads to the rest of the country and even other parts of the world. While some in the convenience and gas station industry act as if this news came out of nowhere, this prediction has been in the air for decades, just as it has been for sugary sodas and tobacco products.

When an industry starts to shift because of cultural movements or regulatory changes, the players within it need to consider moving away from their standard form and shape to avoid outdated stereotypes and overidentification with unflattering associations. Upstarts with little experience, expertise, and capital regularly disrupt established industries because of their ability to develop a new form and shape that taps into these cultural changes while hitting all the right notes with the public.

For instance, let's take a look at the marijuana business. While the cliché pot shops—with their psychedelic array of bongs, pipes, Grateful Dead tapestries, beads, and lava lamps—were in the best position to capitalize on the legalization of recreational weed, they didn't have the right look or modern appeal to attract the mass market, the affluent, or the "Chardonnay Moms." The medical marijuana dispensaries also didn't hit it big with the greater public either with their sterile clinical approach. This is partly because there was still too much of a "hippie" and illegal drug dealer stigma about these recognizable forms and shapes stuck in the public's memories, making potential customers hesitant to venture into them.

But when an outside player from the wellness industry, Adam Bierman, and his partner, Andrew Modlin, came onto the pot scene, they borrowed heavily from two other standard forms and shapes: 1) the sexy design style, look, feel, and layout of Apple Stores and 2) the cool charisma of the hit TV show *Mad Men*. They shifted the image from stoner loner to hipster cocktail lounge and created one of the most recognizable cannabis brands in the nation, MedMen, making them the first pot unicorn to exceed $1 billion in enterprise value. However, like many startups, they encountered many challenging problems, such as navigating the changing regulatory environment and dealing with accusations of mismanagement, corruption, and fraud. These management problems, as unfortunate as they were, didn't invalidate the incredible appeal and market opportunity they created and opened up to the larger public through their new and different retail store design approach. In the hands of a more seasoned operator and management team, they might have become the next Starbucks. Why didn't other established retailers think of this idea? Because they have difficulty letting go of their existing form and shape.

Convenience stores are not alone in this typecasting. Consumers also have fixed ideas and established assumptions about what a grocery store looks like, what they can do inside them, and what problems they solve. For the last fifty years, grocery stores have conditioned customers to think of their venues as a place for people to restock their pantries and refrigerators, but not as a place to hang out, socialize, and have delicious meals with family, friends, and neighbors, despite their proximity to and often central role in neighborhoods.

This focus on getting in and out as quickly as possible made sense during the "super" market growth era because where else were hungry families going to get this shopping done? All grocery stores had to do was worry about beating the competitor down the road. But what if a new wave of outside players from the tech world has a better idea of getting this weekly errand done faster, cheaper, and more conveniently than customers can do now at the traditional grocery store? Now that's a game changer! Or what if the big retail giants can figure out how to sell groceries cheaper with robots, cashier-less checkouts, wired-up carts, free online delivery, and so on? Or what if restaurants come up with appetizing ideas and tasteful techniques for consumers—young, single professionals in particular—to have healthy, gourmet, chef-produced food cheaper than consumers can make at home? As we speak, these are the innovative ideas Silicon Valley tech disruptors, retail giants, restaurant chains, and our firm are working on, and some of these experimental approaches already exist in real-world conditions with impressive results.

Grocery stores are biting their nails about the future disruptions coming down the pike from all angles. So are car dealerships, universities, office buildings, banks, medical practices, malls, and hotels. But all these industries could change their fate and introduce consumers to new offerings if they could just let go of the shackles of their industry's standard form and shape.

LEARNING IS EASY, BUT FORGETTING IS HARD

The retail sectors of grocery, convenience, department stores, and theaters got a lot of mileage from the standard form and shape they pioneered. They should pat themselves on the back for maximizing the life cycle of these recognizable forms and shapes. But the ability to let go and move on to the next break-through is critical because there's a point at which an originally brilliant idea reaches its upper limit of innovation, value, and efficacy. This apex typically happens when an industry matures, the price becomes the primary focus, and it gets harder to impress customers by perfecting the same old best practices. This fatigue eventually happened to the mature market of traditional cell phone and smartphone players like the Motorola Razr and BlackBerry, and it will eventually happen to Apple iPhones if they don't keep breaking new ground and changing standard forms and shapes.

I remind my clients often that "no great market lasts for long." It's not a question of *if* an innovation wave will end but *when*. Organizations must con-stantly look for the next big wave heading their way. No matter how innovative or successful their format might've been for its time, they can't afford to hold on so tightly to their current form and shape forever. Instead, they must pro-actively break free from the industry shackles to create a new model and stan-dard. Blockbuster, Borders, Sears, JCPenney, RadioShack, and Barneys had this opportunity. But they stuck with their current form and shape to their own peril, allowing complete outsiders and industry novices like Apple, Netflix, and Amazon to reinvent the category with a new form and shape that changed customers' perceptions, behaviors, and habits.

GROCERY MISSES ITS MARK

While many areas of the traditional grocery store format and chassis need rein-vention, one area my team and I are particularly interested in is why grocery stores don't borrow, steal, and capitalize more on the success of the form and shape of restaurants, bars, and food halls.

If there is anything distinctive about our current consumer era, it's our passion for talking about food. Our endless need to photograph our meals. Our time-consuming habit of watching cooking shows and our thirst to know where our food comes from, who made it, and what techniques and standards they used to prepare it. This intense interest is unlike anything we have seen in past generations. Despite these food trends and societal shifts, grocery stores still haven't fully capitalized on this massive social phenomenon and cultural movement. (For more insight on these changes, the social scientist Paco Underhill does an excellent job diving deep into this food transformation in his illuminating book *How We Eat*.)

Even though grocery stores are supposed to be in the business of food, very few operators think of food as fashion. They've let their fixation with the commoditization of food by the retail giants and tech disruptors draw their attention away from tapping into the emotional, social, and cultural side of food. Instead of trying to get customers in and out of the store as quickly, cheaply, and efficiently as possible, the industry should be doing the opposite: creating stores customers want to hang out in longer and experience more frequently, just like good restaurants and bars do every day. This is not a random idea but where we see a large portion of consumers heading in the future. The need for humans to break bread together and toast the good life around the theater of food is as old as civilization. Something as common as the pub—or public house—has been in continuous operation since the Roman days and it's not likely to end this year because of Netflix.

COLLIDING WORLDS

In our work with clients as diverse as retailers, orchestras, universities, vacation destinations, and corporate innovation centers, we never fully accept the industry's standard form and shape as an inflexible paradigm we must stay within. Instead, we identify the rules of an industry, determine the limits and frustrations of their boundaries, and then step over the industry fences to see what opportunities lie on the other side.

One technique that helps us accomplish this is colliding one industry's standard forms and shapes with another. This exercise can spark ideas and create the big bang theory we need to achieve a breakthrough. However, we don't conduct these atom-smashing experiments randomly; rather, we look for ideal human behaviors we want to emulate from one industry to graft into our client's industries, which initially seems impossible, if not ridiculous.

In our work with grocery stores, we collide their standard form and shape against restaurants, pubs, farmers markets, food halls, and even food trucks because we want to tap into some of the credibility, authority, and expertise these venues have over traditional grocery stores. Studying the behaviors of these other food models can yield big insights and help us build our case for encouraging our grocery clients to inform customers about their sourcing process and the chef-driven techniques they infuse into their offerings. Showing our clients other successful models outside their industry helps cost-cutting managers realize the importance of small but informative cues like using restaurant-grade tables and upholstered chairs, not the plastic break room furniture most grocery stores use to save money. It gives them insights into why placing the restaurant seating areas near the best views with the most visible and social atmosphere changes the meaning, perception, and purpose of the store as a place to "hang out" with friends and neighbors. It motivates executives to spend the extra few cents to package the food in appetizing containers that communicate a more compelling brand personality as consumers take it home to their tables instead of serving it in utilitarian Styrofoam packaging. It helps grocery store clients shed industry terminology like "prepared food," "produce," and "perishables" and put restaurant-grade uniforms on staff that expresses their passion for food. Even something as simple as the chef's hat, apron, and thermometer in the top pocket become vital brand signals and touchpoints to incorporate into the grocery store experience.

We've used this same kind of highly observant thinking in our work to reinvent the typical corporate innovation center—with its dry, serious, unfun appeal—by colliding it with the hospitality of hip boutique hotels, sassy old-school diners, and the thought leadership mindset of a TED Talk combined with the cultural relevance of a South by Southwest conference. It sounds unlike anything you've seen before, right? That's the point!

The opportunities to collide seemingly disparate forms and shapes together and smash behaviors are endless. When successful, it can jolt customers out of their traditional habits and expectations while inviting them to reconsider a brand-new format and experience. For instance, in the late 1990s we worked for a New York City–based restaurant company looking to expand into the

Carolinas. They had a high-quality pizza product but no name, concept, location, or budget. While they could've gone into any generic strip-center tenant space and called themselves something like NYC Pizza, we worried that wasn't enough to differentiate their product in the market. So we found this old 1920s Pure Oil service station in a redeveloping neighborhood and created a concept called Fuel Pizza Cafe. We built a whole brand story around the language of gas stations, such as "free water and air," "courtesy and prompt service," and "clean restrooms."

The collisions don't always have to be with other built forms; we can sometimes combine them with other cultural norms and phenomena. In the mid-1990s, we developed a restaurant and bar concept that collided the cultural phenomenon of the hit TV shows *Seinfeld* and *Friends* with the societal needs and fears many Gen Xers had in finding suitable partners, buying a home, and starting a family. In that era, there weren't many fast-casual restaurants and options were limited to fast-food joints like Burger King or more formal-dining establishments. Asking for a "table for one," however, at a traditional restaurant and eating by yourself at a two- or four-top table seemed humiliating. The environment did not help facilitate the ability to meet others, as asking other patrons seated at neighboring tables about their food felt like an invasion of privacy. On top of this social discomfort, having to endure the standard structured meal courses of cocktails, appetizers, main meal, dessert, and check didn't fit this generation's eating habits or work/life/gym balance. To counter this, we tapped into a different cultural model and form and shape. We created a restaurant based on living room vignettes—like those we saw on *Seinfeld* and *Friends*. This innovative design approach allowed guests to pop in and out and eat whatever menu items suited their schedule while enjoying the company of a prosocial setting.

Just like being invited to a party at someone's home, we found the living room vignettes were much better than tables for facilitating strangers to meet, talk, and get to know each other better. Much to our delight, customers concentrated on the corners of the vignette layout—say, the sofa armrest next to a chair—and were willing to share these social settings with other customers, creating a shared cocktail party vibe and environment.

In another scenario, we took a premium movie theater chain and collided it with the intimacy of the Emmy-award-winning TV series *Inside the Actors Studio*. The concept entailed creating an insiders' lounge and behind-the-scenes film experience for die-hard movie lovers to hang out with other moviemakers and movie aficionados to enjoy food and drinks while hearing stories that extended the movie-going experience beyond the film.

When a national developer asked us to help them address the popular criticism that shopping centers are just about materialism that preys on younger generations, we studied what parents cared about and cataloged their concerns about childhood development. We experimented with colliding the traditional shopping center site with the standard forms and shapes of a children's museum, a recreational park and nature trail, and a charter magnet school. That exercise gave us the courage to develop a new form and shape that focused on three primary parental concerns of childhood development: the arts, sciences, and sports. And to make the economic business model work, we developed a targeted tenant strategy to attract brands with knowledge in the arts, sciences, and sports—who also wanted to get on the good side of parents—and a new form and shape emerged.

Many standard forms and shapes, such as the mall, grocery store, and convenience store concepts discussed in this book, are long overdue for reinvention. The same goes for the institutions of universities, museums, and performing art facilities. But the most concerning standard forms and shapes needing radical reinvention are office buildings and, by extension, downtown areas, central business districts, and urban employment centers. The rise of technology—combined with the pandemic and the work-from-home revolution—has substantially altered how, when, where, and even why we work and how companies conduct business. The number of office buildings sitting underutilized is troubling. According to global real estate firm JLL, there were 963 million square feet of empty office space at the end of the first quarter 2023. We must also consider the substantial impact on local businesses that historically catered to office workers, such as coffee shops, restaurants, bars, gyms, drugstores, dry cleaners, and sundry shops. As the businesses that serve office buildings and office parks struggle to survive, the need for taxi drivers, valets, security guards, maintenance crews, window cleaners, and parking attendant jobs will continue to decrease. Following the same thread, as revenues from the local tax base lower, undesirable activities, including crime, vagrancy, loitering, and graffiti, will increase.

It's a complicated mess with no easy answers. But instead of mandating employees commute to work like ants during rush-hour traffic to be ware-housed in cubicles invented in another era, we need to accept that our funda-mental patterns of behavior have changed. Our firm has been investigating ways to make the office building a place people want to come to instead of being forced to attend. In this new era of employer/employee dynamics where the best talent calls the shots, the office has to provide a bigger physical, social, and emotional payoff than the work required to go into the office. This new direction has meant smashing the typical office-building paradigm with the standard form and shape of clubs, forts, recreational centers, bars, cafés, hotels, and college campuses. We've also explored how to repurpose office buildings for other uses, such as university, tech hub, and laboratory space, as well as for solving the housing crisis, but these conversions are not as simple as they sound.

The jury is still out on the future fate of underutilized office buildings, but the problem won't fix itself. While writing this book, organizations—such as the American Institute of Architects and the Urban Land Institute—are study-ing the downtown exodus and emigration problem in much greater detail. But it is rapidly becoming a systemic crisis in which the trickle-down effect will impact everyone, from the absence of the tax revenues collected from corpo-rate headquarters downsizing to the funding of roads, ambulances, and public-school programs out in the suburbs. Our political leaders must prioritize this issue as a national concern, as they have in past eras for envisioning highways, dams, airports, water supply, electrical grids, and telecommunications. We need to create a national council and think tank composed of universities, research-ers, urban planners, specialized real estate professionals, and design experts to smash paradigms. We need to explore opportunities to reposition these capital-intensive properties and investments to meet the new reality of how we work today. And we must create a new vision for repurposing Central Business Districts (CBDs) because work today is becoming increasingly decentralized.

SOMETIMES GOING BACK TO AN EXISTING FORM AND SHAPE IS THE ANSWER

My team and I find standard "forms and shapes" throughout society—in diners, barbershops, town halls, and downtowns. But sometimes, they are hidden or harder to recognize and need to be brought more into the light and accepted for their inherent nature. Such was the case for a famous retail shopping district in Santa Monica, California, Third Street Promenade.

Since its inception in the late nineteenth century, Third Street has been the center of business and commerce in Santa Monica. In 1965, though, three blocks of Third Street were converted into a "pedestrian mall," which was an interventionist urban planning concept popular in the 1960s and '70s that entailed closing down the street to vehicular traffic while opening it up to pedestrian foot traffic. The pedestrian mall concept was an intuitive "form and shape" popular in Europe that the U.S. residents quickly picked up on and instinctively knew how to use. But while the idea of people walking and shopping in a car-free environment sounded great, it rarely worked long term. Of the two hundred or so pedestrian malls in the U.S., nearly 90 percent have failed, been shut down, or ripped out entirely.

So why did Santa Monica and other cities try them? As Jacob Ross, a senior associate with the leading real estate consulting practice RCLCO, described in his 2016 article, "Pedestrian malls first emerged in the mid-twentieth century as households and retailers began to suburbanize, leaving those stores and businesses that remained in urban areas to face declining market support. In an attempt to reverse this trend, many cities turned to forms of walkable retail—namely the pedestrian mall—as economic development tools to attract visitors and suburban residents to shop downtown . . . this typology emulated suburban shopping malls, which found success with a park-once approach, and sought to mirror these ideas in an urban setting."

While initially successful, by the 1970s, the then-named Third Street Mall needed yet another intervention or reinvention. Part of the solution was the placement of a new three-level indoor mall—yet another interventionist form and shape—designed by Frank Gehry in 1981 called Santa Monica Place. This indoor mall attempted to capture the spirit of mall culture's steady rise in the country, but its success pulled even more shoppers away from the outdoor pedestrian mall. However, instead of backing away from the promenade concept, the community leaders doubled down and the city approved a $10 million renovation of Third Street.

By the late 1990s and early 2000s, Third Street Promenade became one of the more successful retail districts in the U.S. and was used as a case study and model worldwide. Made initially famous by boutique shops, like the liberal-leaning Midnight Special Bookstore and The Music Box record store (where the actor Jon Cryer did his best impression of Otis Redding in the hit teen movie *Pretty in Pink*), soon enough the national and international flagship stores came with checkbooks in hand to get a piece of the action and street cred, outbidding and displacing the local, funky shops, and with them went the authentic vibe. While it took some time for the decline to set in, the success of the district as a retail destination became a crucial part of its undoing. The tourists that visited the promenade turned off the locals and hipsters from wanting to go to this "tourist trap," as some residents described it. And ironically enough, the well-researched tourists didn't want to go where the tourists went; they wanted to find out where the locals ate, shopped, and hung out, which had moved on to other districts in L.A.

The second factor that affected Third Street Promenade (and SoHo in New York City and many other funky districts in the U.S.) was the steady rise of rental rates compared to waning customer traffic and tenant sales. Slowly but surely, tenants began questioning the cost of their leases and return on investment for locating in the district.

The third problem was the district's approach to improvement became too "professionalized" and strip-mined the funky, edgy-cool factor that made the district unique and distinctive in the first place. Faced with these mounting concerns, the board hired our firm in 2009 to conduct a place brand audit and strategic design review to reposition the promenade.

During our interview process, the constant benchmarks we heard referenced as "goals" or "comparisons" for the district were almost always other malls. The regular complaints centered primarily on the issues of how to address their limited parking options, cleanliness of public bathrooms, and the other undesirable behaviors that are a natural part of any urban environment—all things they proclaimed malls addressed much better than them. There was also one small but interesting gripe and frustration—which became a critical anomaly for us to dig into more—of what to do with the alleyways behind the shops.

When we came back to the group with our findings and recommendations two months later, we started the presentation with one bold, daring set of statements that immediately grabbed everyone's attention and looked like it might get us thrown out for good:

- "No matter how hard you try, you will always be an inferior 'mall.' Why? Because malls are not public places; they're private, for-profit places."

- "But the mantle you can easily own by changing your frame is the most beautiful 'urban district' in the country."

I then explained why the inherent form and shape of the district was that of an urban district, not a mall or shopping street. They had alleys in their district because their history and DNA were that of a real but harder-to-find downtown main street. Their small shop footprints, human-scale facades, sidewalks, curbs, and street widths resulted from being a real downtown, not a mall.

Simply put, Santa Monica's challenge was returning to its roots.

In our professional opinion, they were running the wrong race. Rather than benchmarking other malls, they needed to compare themselves to other urban districts. While their bathrooms and parking situation would never be up to the 5-star standards of what a high-end private mall developer could provide, by most people's standards, they had the best bathrooms and the most reasonable parking solutions of any urban public district in the country.

The problem, however, was in how the leaders framed and referred to the place. For decades they had used words like "pedestrian mall" or "retail shopping district," which conditioned the public to think of it as a mall option among many high-profile developments in the region. But malls and shopping were no longer what people wanted to have associated as part of their image and identity. The more relevant and desirable reflection and cultural terms were found in frameworks such as "downtown," "main street," and "urban district," which, ironically, Third Street was at its core.

While Third Street Promenade was desperately trying to compete on the shiny new standards of the mall amenities, many modern shopping centers, malls, and mixed-use development centers were trying to emulate, simulate, and imitate the authentic grit and quaint character of downtown main streets. The developer of The Grove, Rick Caruso, admits that a big part of his inspiration for his mega-successful development was Third Street Promenade's streets, facade treatments, and sidewalks. But Santa Monica didn't own their inherent urban character and roots with their words, nor did they frame the district with that powerful and relevant form and shape in mind. Using the wrong frame of reference is where many places go off course, but finding the right frame can get places back on the right path to cultural success.

Once we got the board to wrap their heads around these truths, we set out to develop a place brand strategy and conceptual design examples for how the district could reveal more of its true downtown roots and talk less like a private mall developer and more like a real downtown. We even convinced the board to change their historical name from Bayside—which made no intuitive sense to the public, even though Santa Monica is technically a bay—to Downtown Santa Monica, as we intended the name to be a daily reminder to themselves and the public as to what they are.

We suggested the district no longer pursue a national retail/restaurant-only approach but embrace the broader idea of returning to a more comprehensive downtown with a more diverse and local level of work, life, play, and shop activities intermingled, which required some rezoning efforts. We were particularly interested in seeing them bring in creative office spaces to help build a base of daily workers and encourage more service-oriented retail instead of the big national chain or flagship stores. Our goal was to shift the audience from tourist-only to more of a local, diversified crowd.

On June 6, 2018, the leaders of Downtown Santa Monica asked me to make a presentation to the planning commission of the City of Santa Monica, discussing our analysis of the district, which included the critical message of being bold by choosing to be a real downtown and owning their true identity. In the end, the city council approved Downtown Santa Monica's request to create a strategic action plan to reinvest in the Promenade's physical infrastructure. And the reinvention work still goes on today as the district leaders continue to refine, sharpen, and invest in their area with bold visioning and real, substantive changes.

I've found that all urban districts and industries eventually get off course somewhere in their life cycle progression as they max out the limits of one approach and struggle to make the transition to another. While this transition is scary, this fear can be turned into an exciting opportunity to sell the idea of change and course correction to the community of users as a compelling vision. As we see it, urban districts and place brands need to always be about some kind of change, and if positioned with the right frame, this vision of change often sells better than reality. Why? Because vision allows people to get behind the early stages of a cause to make their communities better. It allows them to leave their mark on a place, which is a fundamental human driver, a point we dive into further in chapter eleven regarding the transformation of a blighted urban district.

In the convenience store and grocery store examples, we needed to replace the form and shape with a new one to shift people's expectations to a much broader possibility. However, in the case of the Third Street Promenade district, we needed to go back to the essence of its core form and shape—an original and rare downtown main street—because that's who they were in their bones, and it was something they could own better than anyone, especially the malls. This working village/downtown approach just happened to be what people in society were seeking in their lives. They wanted a genuine downtown and vibrant street life, just as The Grove had created artificially, to help foster a sense of community and allow for more timeless activities of socializing, people-watching, and being a part of a great outdoor room that a scenic place like Santa Monica could provide.

It's essential to recognize that all industries, building types, places, and districts have a unique form and shape, whether hidden or apparent. These standard forms and shapes are typically created by the industry but held in the conditioned memories and experiences of customers who visit the place. Sometimes these forms and shapes are helpful and at other times a limiting factor. One effective way to reimagine them is to think about your place as a theater of life where people see aspects of themselves in the environment and invest their emotions within a choreographed experience, which is a critical skill we will explore further in the next chapter.

CHAP TER SIX

The Theater of Place

"Cinema is a matter of what's in the frame and what's out."

—Martin Scorsese

ONE OF MY FIVE-YEAR-OLD DAUGHTER Kaia's favorite activities is having "Movie Night" with her mom and me. We have hundreds of kids' movies we can stream from the comfort and convenience of our home from the likes of Disney+, Netflix, and Apple TV, and we usually turn these occasions into a little pizza party. Our daughter looks forward to this quality time when she gets her mom and dad's attention to herself. But when the new Minions movie sequel came out, I had a radical idea: "Let's go to the cinema!"

Because of her young age and the pandemic lockdown, Kaia hadn't ever experienced a movie theater. It was a foreign concept to her, and we wondered if she'd get it, much less enjoy it. Much to our surprise, though, from the moment she walked into the movie theater until the ending credits, she was in cinematic bliss and proudly declared on the way home, "I love that place!"

They say movie theaters are dead—a relic of the past. But Kaia knows nothing of their past. She has no nostalgic memories of the big marquee theater on Main Street, and she's unaware of the intellectual debates about whether watching movies at home versus online is better. All she knows is what attracts her attention, ignites her imagination, and makes her eyes light up with anticipation—which I think we all can agree is a beautiful quality.

Ordinarily, Kaia is shy and a bit of a homebody, so we assumed she'd prefer to watch movies in our family room. But, at her insistence, we've seen over two dozen films at the local movie theater since that first experience. Whenever we go inside that magical black box, it's as if aliens have snatched her mind and body. My wife and I don't recognize her because she laughs aloud, claps her hands enthusiastically, shushes me to be quiet, and dances down the aisle during the closing credits music.

Even though I'm in the business of making bonfire moments, it still fascinates me that she intuitively feels the power of seeing movies at a theater without any cultural conditioning or peer pressure. Seeing a movie at home in our pj's is much easier than having to dress up, drive somewhere, and deal with the friction and inefficiency of a place. This convenient experience, however, doesn't compare to the thrill and excitement our daughter gets when she holds her giant bucket of popcorn in her lap, dangles her tiny little feet off the big reclining chairs, and laughs with a group of strangers in this shared storytelling experience.

Many people assume kids today won't want what we had when we were young, such as malls, diners, and movie theaters. But I caution us against ruling these places out entirely. Younger generations have resurrected many things we thought were gone for good, such as homemade ice cream parlors, old-school barbershops, cocktail bars, record players, and main streets. While some write this renaissance off as nostalgia, it's more about course correcting what people want to see in their world in the future.

For instance, as I write this, the Austin-based cinema chain Alamo Drafthouse has committed substantial resources to build and run another relic of the past: a permanent drive-in theater location in Fayetteville, Arkansas. Their reinterpretation of the drive-in includes stand-alone cocktail bars and an outdoor beer garden with a view of the drive-in screen. Our firm had developed similar bold-thinking and innovative strategies for expanding the moviegoing experience in our work for the pioneering cinema chain ArcLight Cinemas. But unfortunately, this legendary Hollywood story didn't end well as they got caught in the pandemic lockdown, which prevented audiences from setting foot inside the cinema and broke the backs and bank accounts of many multigenerational exhibitors.

Although we can have everything we could ever need, want, and desire delivered to our front doors at the push of a button, is that convenience "a good thing"? And is that the kind of future our kids will want? Is it possible that there's something much more primal about going to the movies and coming together as strangers in places that is hardwired into our DNA?

Let's explore that thought.

WATCHING PEOPLE WATCH MOVIES

Some people like to watch movies, but I like to watch people watching movies as part of my job working with theater operators. As a professional voyeur, I like to sense the energy in the room and feel the free fall of silence right before a big eruption of laughter or gasps snatch the audience's emotions. I'm consistently amazed at how a room full of strangers can reach emotional synchronicity and simultaneously wipe tears away from their eyes during a particularly moving scene.

What powerful effects movies have on us! Or, more specifically, what impressive skill directors and cinematographers possess to tap into our feelings and shape our emotional reactions this way!

Most of us aren't consciously aware of the effect movies have on us because directors are so adept at pulling us into their imaginary world that, within seconds, our outside worries evaporate as they control our eyes, capture our attention, and pluck our emotional heartstrings. Most adults walk around trying to suppress their feelings and regulate their emotions to give off the appearance they have things under control. But movies effectively neutralize this instinct to suppress and trigger a specific emotional response and release, which we find ourselves helpless to prevent.

All these emotional and physiological shifts happen without us even realizing what's going on. But it's worth reiterating the experience of watching a film at a movie theater is not a solo experience, like the one at home watching TV, but rather an uninterrupted group experience where complete strangers get in sync with each other's emotions, listen to each other's subtle gasps and sniffles, and participate in a remarkable shared interpersonal experience that resonates across minds and hearts. In repeated studies, scientists have noted listening to stories and seeing movies can induce synchronization between participants' brain activity and heart rate. This phenomenon originates from shared emotions being passed between people, which is a reflection of our inherently social brains. This group experience also reflects the "place participation mystique" and Bonfire Effect we discussed at the outset of this book, where people "participate with each other in a mystical manner, [and] are connected with each other beneath the surface of consciousness." While millions of people may be wired up at the same time to Netflix's global network, we don't feel that same intimate connection with them as we do in theaters.

PLACES AS SCENES OF LIFE

There are many similarities between the power of movies and the power of creating the Bonfire Effect in your place of business. But there's one critical difference: movies aren't real. While the flickering flames of a bonfire are real and can burn your fingers, the flickering images flashing across the screen aren't. At any moment, we could turn around, see the projector, and realize what's happening on the screen is entirely fake and fabricated, an emotional deception of sorts. But why don't we and our fellow audience members turn around to look at the projector in theaters?

First, we enjoy escaping our everyday lives, forgetting about our credit card bills, and getting a break from the episodic events of the 24/7 news cycle. We also like being transported to another time and place and participating in the quest of others because it's therapeutic and inspiring to indulge in a dramatic experience like this. We need this imaginary escape more than we realize.

Secondly, the powerful emotions of tears streaming down our faces, involuntary sounds of laughter, and the genuine heart palpitations we feel in a theater couldn't be more real. The same biological and emotional processes that kick in when we are frightened, being chased, or experiencing heartache get triggered in movies just as they do in real life.

But it's hard to replicate that same kind of powerful, continuous, uninterrupted group experience at home on the couch watching Netflix with the dog barking, teens texting, and the pizza delivery guy ringing our doorbell. Seeing a film in a movie theater captures our full attention, but watching at home gets partial attention, which diminishes the engagement and dilutes the experience. The same could be said of shopping online versus taking a stroll through the local stores on Main Street or listening to classical music on Spotify versus the shared experience of seeing, hearing, and feeling the good vibrations of Beethoven's Fifth Symphony in a majestic concert hall.

COMMANDING ATTENTION

There are many brilliant filmmaking techniques we can adopt to design the experience of places. But the most helpful skill to learn and develop is the deliberate construction of scenes to grab the audience's full attention and never lose it while shaping how they react emotionally to each beat of the film.

Attention is the key word here.

As moviegoers, we are confronted with a tremendous amount of sensory information during a movie. We don't waste our time or energy studying every aspect of the screen or scene. Instead, they rapidly scan, detect, and process the most pertinent details—the gun in the drawer or the shadow in the background. Our human senses are extremely adept at determining what the most critical information is. But the director, set designer, and cinematographer play the biggest role in steering our eyes toward the most vital information blocks they want us to see and the emotions they want us to feel. If that planted object or device is too overt, the film can lose our interest and respect. But if the movie allows us to participate in the action, play detective, and be a part of solving the mystery, we'll stay engaged in the unfolding drama and maintain our heightened curiosity to see how the story turns out in the end.

Many highbrow architects criticize places that are "fake" or "contrived" in their eyes, but audiences don't care if a place is real or fictional. It just needs to be believable and have an emotional frame of reference where we can see aspects of ourselves in the story, participate in the journey and quest, and get in touch with our imaginary identities. That's the job of directors and place-makers: to make us believe in the place and universe they've created, not in an overt conscious or intellectual way, but through an experience where we can be transported to another world and become a character in the story of the place and feel like we're a participant in the brand quest.

"THEME" VS. "RELATABILITY"

Audiences don't like to be disrespected. The overly theme-y concepts of the 1980s and '90s—like Planet Hollywood and Hard Rock Cafe—had their moment, briefly, but eventually they insulted the customer's intelligence and came off as patronizing and shallow. There's a fine line between what's too fake or inauthentic and what the public will accept as believable and credible, or at least not insulting.

For example, Trader Joe's is one of the most respected retail food brands in the U.S. and loved by a loyal legion of customers that we call "bargain gour-mands." With their seafaring name, Hawaiian-themed shirts, and wood pan-eled walls, one would assume they'd get labeled as too themed. Yet, the public buys into their brand proposition hook, line, and sinker. Even though Trader Joe's is owned by a huge international food conglomerate, their stores come off to customers with a local, "aw-shucks" feel and small-town appeal. The author-ity, credibility, and expertise they wield with the public derives from quirky details, such as their consistency in sticking to the brand story on every front, the genuine attitude of cashier-initiated conversations, and even the detailed hand-drawn signs. Trader Joe's understands how to design the theater and sets, while placing the prop devices in just the right way to reflect their brand's values, mission, and storyline. And the staff fit the carefree characters of this shopping adventure perfectly as they perform their improvisational roles without missing a beat.

Finding the right tone and "suspension of disbelief" techniques to get customers to buy into the store experience, products, and brand is tricky. It requires flattering the customers' sense and sensibilities without making them feel stupid, looked down upon, or like pawns in a larger corporate scheme to simply extract dollars from their wallets.

"AUTHENTICITY" VS. "MYTHOLOGY"

Related to this concept of believability is the consumer's continual search for "realness" and human connection. Many experts claim that younger consumers are searching for authenticity. But I'd describe it more as a search for meaning in a world that's losing its mythologies and has become overly concrete, linear, and devoid of spiritual meaning that helps explain the mysteries and struggles in life. And considering that we check our phones, on average, more than 344 times per day—that's once every four minutes—we're pulling further away from making eye contact and having social interaction with other humans, creating a sense of isolation, loneliness, or, as the author Sherry Turkle describes it, being "alone together."

Great places pull audiences into a story full of meaning and mythology, provide a sense of belonging, and help them connect to the mystery of others face-to-face. But to attract them, we have to give them a *payoff* that goes beyond acquiring mere linear transactions and commodities. Thinking about places as theater is critical to the survival and the evolution of places in the future because it provides something the internet, Amazon, Zoom, or TikTok can't replicate.

Over time, my team and I have cataloged a wide variety of physical, social, and emotional factors that play a crucial role in influencing how consumers perceive, interpret, and experience the external world. These insights are not all that different from what directors typically use in making a film or creating a theatrical production. We tell our clients to think of their venues not as "facilities" but as a "live performing arts theater" that has the challenge of attracting audiences to their daily show and allowing them to experience specific emotions within the scenes of a store.

While the process of transforming an everyday place into a performing arts center is no easy task, there are two critical questions we start with to get the producers (clients), directors (designers), and audience (visitors) in the right frame of mind before we turn our attention toward how to "make the scenes." We will continue to use a retail store as an example as it's a place most people are familiar with, but the general logic applies to all places.

What's the Story of Your Store?

Many retail stores lack an overarching story consumers can easily grasp and that taps into their emotions. While retailers tout price, variety, quality, convenience, and service as their big differentiating factors, these aren't emotional appeals but logical assertions and functional equivalents. These rational statements neither move us nor offer something of meaning and belief.

As the social psychologist Jonathan Haidt puts it, "the human mind is a story processor, not a logic processor." So if you want to get into the mind of the public, start with a story. Stories that stir our emotions involve situations that feature both sides of a debate—the good and the bad, the positive and the negative, and the light and dark sides of humanity. Real-world conflict between positive and negative emotions brings up the issue of values, which makes a story engaging.

Provocative arguments around values include the debates between organic versus genetically modified food (Whole Foods) or American-made versus foreign-made motorcycles (Harley-Davidson) or the various concerns about environmental sustainability (Patagonia) that consumers bring up. These kinds of value discussions pull customers into a brand dialogue while placing people on a spectrum of agreeing or disagreeing.

According to a 2023 survey conducted by news outlet Axios and the market research firm Harris Poll, Americans consider Patagonia to have the best reputation of any brand. Patagonia has encouraged consumers to buy used products and to think twice before buying its new products, running a 2011 advertisement headline that read, "Don't Buy This Jacket." The provocative ad brought up the issues of the cost to the environment and suggested consumers reconsider buying a new product in favor of a used one. Ironically, Patagonia saw its revenues grow by 30 percent in 2012, which shows how much talking about real-world values sells.

The best way to find your core story is to start with your company's values because within those beliefs is a hidden gem of an idea about the world that is dying to get out of you. What makes storytelling so attractive is its ability to reveal what people care about, which takes courage. But the companies that disclose what matters to them as human beings are usually far more compelling and captivating to consumers.

If you're having trouble uncovering your company's values, pay attention to what your leaders, managers, or customers are picky about. We're all picky about something, and these issues are worth excavating, highlighting, and exaggerating to see what emerges. Admittedly, this sort of deep probing takes time, interviewing skills, and hyper-awareness, which we'll cover in more detail in chapter seven. But these peculiarities offer us a new path to understanding and a new frame for looking at things while revealing a hidden story of passion, care, and concern worth examining.

Many companies worry their story isn't unique enough. But most storytelling experts will tell you there are only about seven to twelve familiar stories that we repeatedly tell. What matters most is how you tell that story, the setting, and the context. Regardless of how often we've heard them, stories don't have to be new, as much as they need to feel true and relevant to the times. Successful TV shows like *Sons of Anarchy*, *Succession*, and *The Sopranos* draw on old Shakespearean themes, but each one places the story in a different context that hinges on the same core human values.

Stories make us feel like we're on a journey and quest, but they become more engrossing when connected to a cultural moment or movement. For instance, when Whole Foods came out with what we called their "Mother Earth knows best" story and their somewhat veiled, anti–Big Food campaign, their customers got the implicit message and gradually changed how they ate while also putting pressure on the way the traditional food manufacturing industry operates. Likewise, Harley-Davidson's underlying message of free-dom, rebelling, and "sticking it to the man" appeals to cultures worldwide and is still as true today for some riders (and many overworked and stressed-out non-riders) as it was generations ago.

As a visual storytelling firm, the most engaging stories we design come from sorting, sifting, and filtering culture to find the hot-button issues and top-ics of national interest. These stories reveal the ever-changing values, needs, and societal problems that need addressing. We then have to match these findings with our client's story to cast their brand as the protagonist, taking customers on an exciting journey.

We typically find the seed of a perfect story relates to one of the central human quests below:

- Our need to belong to a community

- Our drive to love, nurture, and protect our families

- Our pursuit of fun, laughter, and entertainment

- Our ambition to achieve status, wealth, and prestige

- Our love of art, aesthetics, and beauty

- Our desire to be healthy, and live long, enjoyable lives

- Our thirst for knowledge, insights, and new ideas

- Our desire to feel attractive to others

While this list doesn't represent all the potential story angles, it's an excel-lent place to start thinking about the connection between what you make and what your customers seek in their lives, and what aspects or features have the power to pull consumers deeper into your brand experience.

Where Does Your Story Take Place?

If you want to increase sales, customer engagement, and product experimenta-tion, you need to get customers engrossed in the story of your place. And the real or imaginary location of your story makes a tremendous difference in how credible and believable your storytelling will be. Ask yourself these questions about your story:

- Does your story occur in the past, like a nostalgic rural country store (Cracker Barrel) or down a quaint Parisian street (Le Labo)?

- Or does it happen within the modern, minimalistic aesthetic and distinctive language of Sweden (IKEA)?

- Is it in Texas (Texas Roadhouse), New Jersey (Jersey Mike's), California (California Pizza Kitchen), New Orleans (Pappadeaux Seafood Kitchen), Asia (P.F. Chang's), or Italy (Eataly)? (Even brands like Patagonia, Amazon, and Sierra Nevada use geographic brand names to communicate their perspective, personality, and mystique.)

- Does your story happen in a warehouse (Costco) or among a band of carefree traders out at sea (Trader Joe's)?

- Or perhaps this story takes place in someone's elegantly designed home (Restoration Hardware), on an urban, graffiti-filled street (Urban Outfitters), or at a carefree resort island (Tommy Bahama or Jimmy Buffett's Margaritaville)?

While some of these concepts are dated, I use them for broad recognition as the settings, props, and scenes inside these mini-universes help transport us to a vivid time and place.

Designing these brand realms requires bold imagination, creative exploration, and brave experimentation to go beyond the literal and utilitarian world into the mythical places of our imagination. To locate the imaginary places of our clients' stories, we assemble a "Field of Meaning," which allows us to gather a galaxy of artifacts, icons, and symbols that serve as portals into a client's quest and help set the stage for a meaningful story to spring forth.

At first, we don't judge these artifacts as much as we try to catalog all of them. But eventually, we have to select just a few pivotal pieces to focus on. To help with this editing process, we imagine we're doing live theater and can only use a few strategically placed props to establish the scene. Using this technique, we ask ourselves:

- What key props and background items do I need to deploy to get the audience in the right frame of mind for the story?

- What key pieces can help communicate the values and reinforce the moral of the story?

- What components would lend themselves best for creating a sense of anticipation and foreshadowing for the story?

Once we've identified the most critical symbols, props, and artifacts, we can find the patterns for how all the pieces are interconnected and why they make sense together as a visual language. After some time and exploration, we usually find these props are part of a larger sub-world (real or imagined), which we call the "brand realm." Whereas props focus on the story's micro-setting (a specific scene), the larger place where all these props exist in the world or universe is the realm of our story. If you're fortunate to have both a brand realm and the right props, your story will be much more captivating and rewarding for customers to experience. For example, in the show *Mad Men*, the realm was the legendary Madison Avenue in New York and the props were all the forgotten but nostalgic items like typewriters, pay phones, slide show projectors, fedora hats, and Lucky Strike cigarettes, which helped transport us into their world.

Successful retail stores like Williams Sonoma (a Napa Valley kitchen, perhaps a winery), Anthropologie (a well-traveled, nostalgic attic), Le Pain Quotidien (a French/Belgium country store), Kiehl's (an old-time apothecary shop), Eataly (Italian farmers market), and Wegmans (an Italian market street and piazza) all do a wonderful job of placing their stories in a robust realm and evocative setting with expertly curated props, wardrobe pieces, and a uniquely defined Field of Meaning. Sure, the products these stores offer could exist in a stripped-down warehouse store, like Bed Bath & Beyond, for much cheaper. But that kind of bleak treatment would reduce their value, meaning, and emotional capacity, turning them into common commodities customers could easily find and purchase online.

Consumers have demonstrated their desire to enter these kinds of consumer fantasies and places of imagination. They've also proven their willingness to pay a slight premium to include the meaning and experience of the setting as part of the overall purchase equation because it makes shopping an enjoyable, fun, recreational, and therapeutic way to escape everyday life.

Steps one and two are determining the story our clients should tell and where that story takes place. But the superglue that binds audiences to your content hinges on the art and craft of making the scene, which requires studying the best of the best.

THE PRINCIPLES OF MAKING A SCENE

Many film buffs consider Hitchcock one of the greatest movie directors of all time. As the master of suspense and a pioneer in scene-making, his iconic films like *The Birds*, *Psycho*, and *North by Northwest* held our full attention while also scaring the bejeezus out of us by hijacking our biological operating systems and emotional response mechanisms.

One of Hitchcock's most significant contributions to filmmaking was his ability to elicit specific emotions from viewers by carefully crafting and choreographing each scene. The secret to emotions, he believed, was "in the shot," by controlling what the viewer sees with their eyes and feels with their emotions.

Whenever I'm stuck on a design assignment, whether it's a supermarket, restaurant, or orchestra facility, I ask myself, "How would Alfred Hitchcock design this place?" Looking at these places through Hitchcock's lens helps my team and me storyboard the overall experience from a more dramatic human perspective instead of thinking of the space in linear feet and inches of inventory. It's unlikely Hitchcock would tolerate our industry's preoccupation with floor plans, sections, elevations, material sample boards, or planograms. Instead, he'd break down the space into critical scenes while loading them up with psychological meaning and cultural values that pulled audiences in and made them feel a specific emotion. These feelings would not be vague, incidental, or left to chance but deliberately and intimately related to a value he wanted you to feel, first in your gut, beating heart, and sweaty palms, then in your reflective mind and emotional memory. Much like how Hitchcock got us to think twice when screeching birds fly over our heads (*The Birds*) or when we

see a shadow through a steamy shower curtain (*Psycho*), he'd make us feel specific emotions about the situation and environment. Of course, he'd tie these
sensory-rich scenes seamlessly together into the larger moral of the story and an
archetypal quest similar to that of a brand quest.

Instead of looking at places as facilities with departments, we look at them
as a series of intimate scenes visitors feel with their senses and experience with
their emotions. Over the last few decades of studying audience reactions to our
productions, we have distilled the art and science of scene-making in places
into five guiding principles.

1. A Good Retail Scene Has a Beginning, Middle, and End

Most retailers don't create scenes in their stores as much as they provide functional access to an inventory of products through aisles, shelves, or zones. Or
if they have scenes, they are usually too numerous and disconnected for the
customers to comprehend. Ideally, you want to organize products into a series
of coherent scenes that attract the shopper and pull them into a larger journey
through your store and brand. The goal of each scene is to make the customer
want to know more about what is inside the frame of view.

One way to pull customers from one scene to the next is to imagine a chain
of scenes representing the store's overall experience from beginning to end.
Every link in the chain is vital to customer flow, engagement, and integrity.
All it takes, however, is one bad, incoherent, and disjointed scene in the chain
to lose the viewer's interest and dilute the strength of the entire story. As the
acclaimed and prolific filmmaker Steven Soderbergh said, "the key to making
good movies is to pay attention to the transition between scenes. And not just
how you get from one scene to the next, but where you leave a scene and where
you come into a new scene. Those are some of the most important decisions
that you make. It can be the difference between a movie that works and a
movie that doesn't."

Great films keep us on the edge of our seats from beginning to end because
of their ability to edit out scenes and moments that don't make sense or lose the
viewer's eye or interest. A legendary director like Ridley Scott of the film *The*

Martian (2015) shot 250 hours of raw film footage before facing the daunting task of editing all that film down to a concise 144-minute story. And David Fincher shot 500 hours of film footage to get to a 149-minute movie, *Gone Girl* (2014). While a lot of good material falls on the cutting room floor, the editing process is where the brilliance happens because audiences have limited time and attention spans. The same goes for creating engaging places.

Many stores we tour get the critical first scene, or what we call the "arrival scene," wrong right off the bat. By wrong, I mean the scene is not framed in a way that immediately grabs our eye, pulls us into the store, and tells us something vitally important about the brand story we're about to experience by shopping at this place. Instead, customers usually see half of the produce department, a quarter of the floral department, and maybe another quarter of the cereal aisle. None of these partial views of scenes are compelling, alluring, or coherent, forcing us into a rational, get-in-get-out-of-the-store mentality.

The first scene of a movie, like the first sentence, paragraph, and page of a book, is critical to setting the stage and getting you to engage with the story. If that opening page or scene is not right, we'll lose the audience's interest in taking the next step. Successful writers will tell you each page has to be so good and tempting that it entices you to flip to the next page; the same is true of stores, zone by zone. Each corner, vista, or side aisle glimpse has to be so enticing that it keeps pulling you deeper into the scene. While that might sound like a high standard, that's the job of moviemakers and place-makers.

Humans tend to remember how something starts and finishes the most, which is especially true in retail, but operators and designers regularly overlook these critical scenes. People also tend to remember their best, peak experience inside a store, such as the bread-making or dessert stations at a Wegmans, and their worst experience, like waiting in long lines at the checkout zone of poorly designed stores.

Memory plays a much more critical role in defining how people think about your place and what they expect from the experience, such as dread or excitement. Stores with bad memories can be improved and enhanced by crafting the scenes properly, but this requires designing the store using the frame of scene development, not functional floor plan layouts or merchandising planograms.

2. A Good Retail Scene Has a Mini-climax Inside of It

Like a movie, something memorable, revealing, or dramatic should happen inside each scene of the retail store. We call this critical part of the scene the "mini-climax."

A mini-climax for a scene, say in the Wegmans grocery store example I used previously, could be the pizza guy (actor) in his white pizza outfit and hat (costume/wardrobe) throwing the pizza dough in the air (action) while another person takes a giant wooden paddle (prop) off the old redbrick wall (setting) to pull out a piping-hot pizza from the wood-burning stove while shouting, "Freshly baked pizza!" (drama).

For Freson Bros., discussed in chapter two, we designed several scenes strategically placed throughout the store. One of the more memorable scenes is a sub-brand module called Mother Dough Bread Co. The bakers (actors) wear distinctive uniforms (costume/wardrobe) while kneading (action) dough, crafting cinnamon buns and tending to racks (prop) of freshly baked bread.

These little scene hooks and dramatic moments provide vital contextual cues about the values of the brand's story while also capturing the customer's attention in imaginative and memorable ways. More importantly, it gets the customer's focus off the commodity issue of price and into the dramatic issues of quality, process, and care.

Although much trickier, the center aisles of grocery stores also have many opportunities to create mini-climax moments, like what our firm did for Nabisco by creating a brand realm we called "Mom's Kitchen" right in the cookie and cracker aisle that I described in chapter three. This Norman Rockwell/Martha Stewart–inspired scene was intentionally designed to remind customers of the meaningful rituals and traditions around the timeless wisdom of Mom's kitchen table and the role cookies and crackers played in making that memorable scene for the family.

The opportunities for defining the mini-climax for each department in a retail store are limitless. That's where the creativity and connectivity to the brand story comes in to tie back to a brand's core values. These peak experiences can leave a lasting impression and positive memory in the customers' minds.

3. A Good Retail Scene Reinforces the Overall Plot, Quest, and Story of the Brand

On average, a successful retail store should have between five and eight major scenes that make up the whole store experience, each imparting something unique about the department they represent.

To create a cohesive and naturally flowing brand experience, each of the scenes of a retail store needs to contribute to the brand's larger plot, quest, and moral. But underneath these scenes are the deeper core values of what the retail brand stands for and the company's processes and editing philosophy to bring customers these product offerings. Like the protagonists in a movie, your customer should care about the processes and root for your brand to overcome the odds of fighting some villain and becoming victorious in their quest to succeed. This quest must be a mutually shared journey between the customer and the brand. And the store staff (actors) should fit the part of joining that cause and serving as the Yoda or sage that provides the right advice or shines a light on the path we need to take. The customer must see themselves in the story quest of where the brand is heading.

Costco does this by making the customer feel like they cut out the middleman (villain) and are bringing wholesale products and prices directly to the customer. Some of the most important props and signals Costco uses are warehouse buildings, massive metal shelving racks, plain concrete floors, and a loading dock mentality. Despite their impression, these components are not used as much for efficiency or frugality as they are key signals to the customer of their brand story and consumer value proposition of wholesale prices. As one Costco executive put it to me, "It costs us a lot of money to look this cheap!"

Trader Joe's does this by convincing consumers their buyers have scoured the earth looking for perfectly delicious finds that won't break the bank. Some of the most vital scene-making props and signals Trader Joe's uses are tropical shirts, handwritten signs, and unsophisticated wood paneling that make them seem like a funky, local neighborhood store instead of being owned and managed by a large, multinational conglomerate.

4. A Good Retail Scene Has Carefully Chosen Props, Cues, and Triggers

Whenever audiences encounter a scene in a film or a store, they subconsciously try to make sense of it in the blink of an eye. Why don't people engage longer in a scene? Because the brain runs on a limited power source, equivalent to about a sixty-watt light bulb, and it won't wear itself out on things that aren't essential to our survival or can potentially enhance our lives.

For the Nabisco scene, we had to grab customers' eyes quickly and get them in the right mood to focus on cookies and crackers. By deploying strategically placed cues and triggers—such as the cookie tins, rolling pins, kitchen tiles, picnic patterns, and cabinet drawers—we significantly increased customer engagement and sales of these products. One manager, however, tried to strip these pivotal details out to save money, particularly the drawer pulls. He didn't realize these tiny yet potent details would reduce the emotional pull and meaning of the scene.

The visual digestion of scenes has to happen quickly, as customers don't have the time, energy, or attention span to decipher complex scenes, particularly when there are other distractions, such as people, carts, sounds, smells, and so on vying for their attention. Emotionally rich, potent, and symbolic props shorten these time frames immensely.

5. A Good Retail Scene Has Values and Says Something About What You and Your Customers Care About

The form of a book is different from, say, a movie. Whereas a book consists of 50,000–75,000 words on average and may take a couple of days or weeks to read, a movie based on a book must be greatly condensed into 90 to 120 minutes, allowing audiences to view them in one sitting. So how do screenwriters go about the challenging task of turning a book into a movie?

They have to identify the key scenes in the book that impart the most important values about the protagonist's (the brand's) quest. Then they must determine if the reader (customer) will care enough about those values and that quest to stay engrossed in the story until the closing credits.

The retail store experience is not all that different.

While the retail strategy might take all day to present to executives in a conference room, the store experience must capture and communicate a set of values and brand quest in a short amount of time. Of course, these values must be something customers can care about.

Good movies often present a topic we're not sure we'll initially agree with or care about. But through presenting and telling the story just the right way, we find ourselves immersed in the drama and caring about something we didn't know would mean so much to us. (I felt this way about *Inception*, *Moneyball*, and *Black Swan*.)

Whole Foods did this for many customers in the 1990s and early 2000s. While there were loyal customers who got Whole Foods from day one, many more non-customers didn't understand the value of what the brand offered. These non-customers—essential to the brand's future growth potential—didn't know why they should pay more money for hard bread with no preservatives or hormone-free meats that didn't have robust flavors or biodegradable detergents.

The incredibly seductive theater of retail scenes Whole Foods created in their stores, however, did an excellent job of converting people to their way of thinking by getting them to experience something they didn't know they could care about. While many other natural and organic food stores had been around long before Whole Foods arrived, they didn't create enticing scenes and persuasive theater that convinced the non-customers to see why these products had value and were worth paying a slight premium to acquire. Many great scenes come to mind when thinking about the early days of Whole Foods, such as the way they told visual stories in the produce department about the local farmers they worked with, their produce butcher stations, and how they encouraged customers to sit down and eat, drink, and hang out in the store. But the one scene that sticks out to me the most is the Health and Beauty department. At the time, we were used to going to Safeway or Kroger and wading through shelves of Crest, Listerine, and Dial soap packages. But Whole Foods dropped customers into a foreign experience surrounded by unfamiliar products their parents never had in the medicine cabinet and presented them with an opportunity to ask a wise shaman (employee) who offered thousand-year-old tonics and tree bark to cure common illnesses versus NyQuil and Vicks cough drops.

LIFE IS LIVED IN SCENES

Hitchcock believed it's intuitive to visualize and think of life in imaginative scenes. But as we "grow up" and become more linear and rational in our thinking, especially in business, we often lose our connection to that imagination. Suppressing our imagination leaves us thirsty for explanations beyond what the provable world can provide. While religion, spirituality, and other belief systems provide some of this meaning, great movies, experiences, and places can affect us profoundly—and so can the store experience.

Understandably, most retailers are nervous about the new world reality confronting commerce today, as they should be. But the key for retailers is not to compete on the same utilitarian dimensions or playing field that commodity players excel at. To survive and thrive in the future, brick-and-mortar retailers must reconsider what they are selling and shift the retail game to a different value equation and payoff that goes beyond price, variety, and convenience.

Based on all that we see happening in retail today with the profusion of online replacements, we believe the physical stores that define the future will infuse their product offerings with other equally important features, such as meaning, entertainment, socializing, adventure, discovery, leisure, and belonging. The value proposition will have to go beyond the literal product itself and satisfy other consumer needs, wants, desires, and quests, for which there are many.

Despite how advanced the world is today, humans never tire of good storytelling. If anything, we need meaningful stories now more than ever to make sense of our seemingly chaotic world and provide some hope and explanation in an increasingly uncertain environment. People are actively looking for good storytellers to shine the light on the future path. Today's businesses and institutions have a tremendous opportunity to provide helpful answers, advice, and insights while creating an invigorating experience and theater of place that taps into consumer emotions through the art, craft, and science of storytelling.

To make that happen, let's dive into Part III of this book. We will turn the theory of the last four chapters into action through a detailed breakdown of our innovative place-making system that has the power to turn your brand's story into an enchanting Bonfire Effect that audiences will eagerly crawl through mud to participate in.

PART THREE

How to Build Your Own Bonfire

"I fear not the man who has practiced 10,000 kicks once, but I fear the man who has practiced one kick 10,000 times."

—Bruce Lee

I'M A STRATEGIC ARCHITECT BY day, but most weeknights, you can find me trying to pick myself up off the mat after getting my legs swept out from underneath me by a small, unassuming, sixty-eight-year-old man at a Muay Thai kickboxing gym in Hollywood.

I've been training with the masters of this ancient Thai martial arts form for the last twenty-five years. This passion isn't necessarily about self-defense; it has more to do with my love of learning about human behavior. And there's no better place to see how humans behave than when grappling with the panic signs of our "fight or flight" instincts inside the ring. It's the perfect raw material to take me away from work yet put me right back into it.

Before you get some mental image of me as a ripped Van Damme–looking tough guy, let me bring you back to reality. At 5'8", 165 pounds, slightly balding with a pooch, and wearing dad jeans, I'm about as ordinary and unassuming as a person can get. Nobody would ever mistake me for a fighter, much less a gym regular, but having this martial arts software installed in my operating system gives me quiet confidence. I rarely worry about taking care of myself in most situations. This confidence is because I have a "system of response" to address external factors that my instructors have drilled so deeply into my muscle memory I don't have to think about what I'd do in a fight, as my body knows how to respond automatically. That's the beauty of having a reliable system—it gets the indecisive, overthinking, pausing brain out of the way and lets the body's natural but practiced response mechanism react without the conscious mind slowing things down.

Having an automatic system of response is not only critical in martial arts; it's also essential in designing, building, and managing successful places. While architecture has a "system," it's based primarily on the laws of aesthetics, such as symmetry, composition, proportion, etc. There's also a system in business based on the laws of economics, marketing, and management. What most organizations lack, however, is a system of place that considers the psychological, sociological, and strategic dimensions of how to attract people to their place in an ever-changing world while surviving competitive attacks from the retail giants and tech disruptors. Far too many organizations are forced to use an old real estate playbook and archaic design doctrines developed before the internet came onto the scene and unleashed the new era of the Replacement Economy. Everything from milk, art, therapy, and dating can be acquired without the need to visit a place.

These organizations also don't realize the criticalness of using speed and timing as a strategy to stay ahead of these monumental shifts barreling down on our culture. As a result, when faced with competitive threats or sudden consumer shifts, many established organizations pause, debate, set up task force committees, and get caught in analysis paralysis. When this happens, their more nimble and agile competitors find a hole in their defense system and exploit this weakness by picking off the most vulnerable customers.

"Your goal in the ring is to turn your opponent into your assistant," my martial arts instructor jokes. "And you do this by baiting them to move where you want them to go and getting them to fight on your terms, not theirs." Sadly, many local and regional stores become the assistants to retail giants like Walmart and tech dynasties like Amazon by trying to play their game instead of leveraging their own inside advantage. They get lulled into the open battlefield of price, variety, and convenience and then get hammered by their more efficient systems, massive reach, and immense investment capacity, allowing them to give away products at a loss for other indirect gains, such as Prime memberships. But the smaller retailers don't have to play this game. Instead, they can run their own race and win by providing a different product, such as a higher level of delight, social engagement, and leisure.

Despite his legendary status and sixty years of training, my instructor still takes weekly classes at other martial arts schools. When I ask him why a legendary guru needs to visit no-name dojos, he reminds me he's a lifetime student of martial arts. "The more I learn about martial arts, the less I know," he says with half a century of wisdom, scars, and experience under his belt.

I've been a lifetime student of the business of place-making and place-branding. The more I learn about psychology, sociology, cultural anthropology, biology, neuroscience, branding, and the design of places, the more I realize how much we still have to learn, uncover, and incorporate into our system. While some might find this process overwhelming, my team and I believe in an open system of continual learning and adapting our system to meet new types of competitor threats and consumer shifts. Because we practice it daily, it's a permanent part of our muscle memory.

Our system entails a standard five-step process: extract, distill, articulate, crystallize, and maximize. We'll go over four of those steps in this book. However, we won't be covering the crystallize phase in detail as it's very visual and warrants an entire book of its own. In short, the crystallize phase is the creative act of manifesting written strategy into experiential design concepts and ultimately into tangible form and shape. Throughout this book, though, we have sprinkled numerous examples of how to turn complex ideas into symbols, icons, and scenes that have the power to convene people in places.

In the following four chapters, I will unfold the comprehensive system we've developed that has allowed our clients to retain or regain their edge over outside influences for the last three decades. This system is full of proven techniques to help you and your organization survive surprise attacks and withstand the constant barrage of perpetually changing market conditions.

CHAP TER SEVEN

Extract

"It is not the answer that enlightens, but the question."

—Eugène Ionesco

THE EXTRACT PHASE DRAWS OUT the knowledge, wisdom, and insights our clients have within them—conscious or not—about their business, industry, customers, and competitors.

Knowing where to start a complex innovation assignment can be daunting, if not paralyzing. From experience, though, we know we'll hit upon the big breakthrough ideas we need if we stick to our system and patiently explore the five fields of discovery detailed below:

- Management interviews
- On-site observations
- Competitor reconnaissance

- Background explorations on the edges of the industry
- Cultural conversations

FIELD 1: MANAGEMENT INTERVIEWS

Many companies we work with have entire departments, floors, and sometimes separate buildings dedicated to research. As part of the "onboarding" process, they'll send us reams of confidential reports before walking us through numerous PowerPoint presentations to help us get our arms around their brand, customers, competitors, and the various constituencies involved. As useful as we find this information, it rarely gives us the creative spark to create the game-changing ideas and innovative breakthroughs required to leap into the future. However, watching, listening, and observing people inside and outside their organizations always gets us there.

For this reason, we start each assignment by removing our creativity hats and pulling out our detective notepads to conduct interviews with the management team. Depending on the organization's size, we typically interview anywhere from six to sixteen managers directly involved in the enterprise's strategic direction. Like therapists, we must prioritize listening over talking to get our clients comfortable revealing their hopes, dreams, fears, and aspirations for their brand. We must also make them feel comfortable and safe enough to reveal their organization's mishaps, misfires, and missed opportunities. All of this information contains vital insights that help us understand the narrative journey of their company, where it's been, and where it needs to head next.

While there is some degree of "just the facts" information we need to collect, the most revealing questions we ask circle around three specific areas:

1. Where is your company and industry most limited, constrained, and frustrated?
2. Where are your customers most limited, constrained, and frustrated by what the company and industry offers?
3. Where are your managers/employees most limited, constrained, and frustrated by the company and industry?

The answers to these questions will vary depending on who we ask. But with enough interviews, a pattern always emerges showing us where to look for the big ideas. While most of these leads will turn into dead ends, there's always one small anomaly someone says that allows us to crack the code of where the company and industry should head next.

The secret to uncovering breakthrough ideas and unlocking the future potential of a brand starts by tapping into the embedded wisdom, experience, and expertise organizations already possess. We typically find that most clients already know what they need to do but could use some coaxing and coaching to get it into a coherent plan that builds their confidence. Understandably, most clients get caught between two lands: the safety, comfort, and nostalgia of the past and the uncertainty and risk of the future. Our job is to get them through that ocean of doubt to find safe passage to more abundant opportunities.

Many design consultants are anxious to change things to make them their own, but this overconfidence can further confuse managers, dilute brand clarity, and lead to problems with strategic coherency. Most organizations I encounter don't suffer from the lack of good ideas but the ability to get them through their committee structure, leadership maze, and bureaucracy with any degree of integrity or conviction. Instead of more ideas and solutions, most organizations need help editing and sharpening the best ideas, solutions, and strategies from their portfolio of options so they can focus their resources toward pursuing a clear and convicted path.

FIELD 2: ON-SITE OBSERVATIONS

Odd as it sounds, it's not uncommon for my team and me to pull out lawn chairs and sit inside or outside our client's venue for days during our initial observation period. Like trying to catch fish when they don't appear to be biting, we'll wait patiently for the big insights to swim by and reveal their hidden flash of brilliance—which they always do, assuming we're willing to wait long enough to catch a brief glimpse of them.

However, my biggest struggle with designers is getting them to stop designing solutions before they've identified the problem through patient observation.

As the "experts" in design, they can't help but want to show clients what they can do, but as Frank Lloyd Wright said, "An expert is a man who has stopped thinking because 'he knows.'" I regularly remind them the big fish insights won't bite until we prioritize watching and listening over proposing rapid-fire solutions in search of a problem to solve. Only then can we decode the hidden patterns and connections of everything around us, including customers' shoes, clothes, walking patterns, eye movements, body language, facial gestures, social interactions, and so on. Sometimes it takes days for these anomalies to appear and a clear pattern to emerge. But once we get a few insights nibbling on the line, a whole boatload of them begin to rise to the surface.

We typically start with the following ten preliminary questions to get our observation pumps primed. For ease of discussion, I'll use a retail store as the example. But with a few adjustments, the questions apply to most other industries we work in.

1. How Do Customers Walk into Your Store?

We start our observations in our client's parking lot or on the sidewalk to watch how people walk into the store. We do this for two reasons. First, by studying their body language and facial expressions, we can usually tell if they're anxious, excited, hurried, tired, irritated, or relieved to be there, which sets the stage for their overall experience. Second, by gauging their emotional state, we can determine what mindsets they bring into the store and how we can help make their day a little easier, brighter, or more enjoyable.

2. How Do Customers Walk Once Inside Your Store?

Some customers walk with a fast, determined gait and a sense of urgency to get in and out of the store as quickly as possible (which means the store hasn't done a good job of dividing their intentions and making their surroundings engaging enough to grab their attention). Others walk slower and take their time to pull products off the shelves to read labels. Some people look straight ahead and walk with a twenty-foot gaze, blowing by everything next to them, while others have a two-to-four-foot gaze, resulting in more interaction and engagement with the offerings. And some people want to get to one particular area of the store and dispense with the rest of the experience.

Once we uncover these patterns of walking behaviors inside the store, these observations help us understand customers' mindsets, how the store enhances or impedes their engagement levels, and where to consider making the necessary adjustments.

3. Which Areas of Your Store Do Your Customers Not Visit or Experience?

Regardless of the store size, customers often don't walk every inch of the sales floor. This underutilized space should concern operators, but many are unaware of where this happens.

Customers typically swim with their eyes and paddle with their feet to the specific areas that interest them and avoid or ignore the rest, which is not good for the store or the products inside those zones or aisles. Determining these "hot zones" and "dead zones" is critical to understanding what's working and what areas need more attention and design development.

4. Where Do Customers Appear to Be Engaged or Disengaged in Your Offering?

Customers engage with certain parts of stores more than others. In almost every retail chain we work with, we'll find dead zones that are underutilized and inefficient regarding sales per square foot. We sometimes use sophisticated technological tools such as "heat maps." But overall, these tools aren't as illuminating as the human eye and powers of observation.

Many retailers assume a larger store will generate bigger sales, but we can help them gain a better ROI by showing them how to recapture and revitalize the dead zones to increase the effectiveness and engagement of those underperforming areas. One of the early pioneers and masters of analyzing, decoding, and interpreting store behavior is Paco Underhill, the founder of Envirosell. We consider his books—such as *Why We Buy, How We Eat*, and *Call of the Mall*—essential reading and recommend our clients use his services and insights when they can.

5. In Which Areas of the Store Are Customers More Social or Antisocial?

Customers react to people differently in different parts of the store. They also exhibit different social attitudes and behaviors depending on how conducive the environment is for facilitating prosocial behaviors.

For instance, in grocery store cafés and wine departments, customers will talk casually with other customers and share ideas about the products. But in checkout zones, they can become anxious, uncivil, and easily agitated by those who leave too much space in the line and are not "closing the gap." These people didn't miraculously change who they were; the environment changed how they felt and behaved toward one another. This change is not unlike the stress that drivers exhibit merging onto a busy highway from a congested on-ramp or that travelers reveal tapering into a disorganized single line during the crowded airline boarding process.

Social cooperation is stressful, and standing in the checkout line within a tight, narrow, and awkward space where people feel they have little control makes them even more anxious and irritable. Fix those environmental stressors, and you'll change the behavior and reduce the tension affecting customers' perception and memory of a place.

6. Who Do Your Customers Shop With?

Customers who shop alone behave differently than those who shop with their kids, spouses, partners, friends, or extended family. When parents shop with their children, they often include them in the shopping process and teach them about food, money, value, and meals, which is fascinating to watch. When adults shop with their partners or extended family, they have the potential to turn their shopping experience into a leisure activity that's fun and social, assuming the store creates an environment that promotes and encourages this activity. In some chains, customers even dress up to go to their stores and make a special day of it.

Why does this matter? Because task-oriented shopping promotes a commodity mindset, which today's internet does better than most brick-and-mortar stores. But shopping with friends and family adds an in-person social interaction advantage the internet can't match and it leads to much higher sales.

7. Where Do Customers Seem Delighted Versus Frustrated?

Most of us know when our friends, family members, and bosses are mad, irritated, or uncomfortable because it's written all over their faces. You can also see these feelings expressed in customers' body language while shopping. They'll shrug their shoulders when confused and look away when it's socially uncomfortable. On the flip side, their eyes will light up when they see something they like or are interested in studying further.

We look for these moments of excitement to better understand how the store generates an enthusiastic response. We also look for moments of frustration to better understand where the store experience is lacking and failing to engage customers.

8. Which Patterns Do We See in Customers' Cars, Shoes, Clothing, Etc.?

Intentional or not, my team and I believe everything communicates and is an important sign or signal. For this reason, we pay a lot of attention to the cars customers drive and the shoes, jewelry, watches, and clothes they wear. If most customers drive pickup trucks, listen to country music, wear jeans and boots, and walk out with a six-pack of Budweiser over Heineken, it says one thing. But if customers drive luxury sports cars while wearing yoga outfits and munching on kale chips and granola bars, it says another.

Even though these observations may seem obvious, you'd be surprised by how many business leaders and designers don't notice, much less track and catalog, these potent signals. More importantly, they don't drill down deeper into the issues of identity and dreams these signals reflect in customers. They see them as function and utility, not aspirations. But watches don't just tell time; they also serve as signals to others about who we are and what identities we desire to project to the world. A fancy Rolex watch says one thing about the wearer, whereas a thrifty Timex or colorful Swatch says another. The store environment should reflect an identity the customers proudly want to wear. As the illuminating author Benjamin Lorr points out in his fascinating book *The Secret Life of Groceries: The Dark Miracle of the American Supermarket*,

> The holy grail of American taste seems to be the type of person whose individual taste is both an expression of them as an individual and one that is socially approved—two ideas that are by definition in tension—and thus taste and consumption itself is bound up in a paradox of sorts. Freedom to express the unique self but requiring approval from the greater conforming community, which itself is tied up in an even greater paradox: We believe we are individuals with an essence, that does not depend on material objects, but if that essence or sense of individuality is ever going to mean anything, if it's ever going to be demonstrated to our social group, then possessions and material objects are one of the few effective means of showcasing it.

9. Which Customers Stand Out the Most?

Most brands we work with have a core customer base that fits a standard audience profile they expect to see in their stores. But the customers we're most interested in investigating further are those that don't fit that typical profile and seem out of place in the store because they often depict an adjacent market segment that the brand might be able to attract and reach. These "potential customers" also represent a significant growth opportunity for our clients if we can adjust the store's appeal and meaning slightly to make them feel more comfortable and connected to the brand.

10. How Do They Walk Out of the Store?

The real scorecard moment for us to watch is how customers walk out of the store. If they look beat down, haggard, and worn out, it's a good sign the store environment and experience have drained their energy. What's draining them? It could be the lights, sounds, materials, traffic flow, signage, people, or other stimuli. We aim to get to the bottom of those factors to learn more about how the store experience affects them.

On the other hand, if they walk out excited, inspired, and animated, as they do at Wegmans, Apple, and Bass Pro Shops, we know we're helping to fill their tanks with energy. And, of course, we zero in on which aspects of the store experience contributed the most to these positive emotions.

As much invaluable information as we glean from noticing the subtle behaviors of humans, we also extract tremendous insights by studying the design logic and design decisions of existing environments. Whether coordinated or not, all kinds of people have their hands in making lasting decisions and impressions about places such as those found in cities and urban districts. The roadway locations, sidewalk widths, streetlamp styles, and the urban furniture scattered throughout a city all contribute to an overall perception and pattern language. Of course, we take note of the obvious design gestures in the foreground—such as the civic centers, museums, and public art installations—but it's the small anomalies happening in the background that are often more revealing. Being told to pay attention to things you don't normally pay attention to sounds odd, but the art of learning how to see your environment is noticing the small background details we typically take for granted because of our overfamiliarity with an environment or our dominant impression of foreground landmarks.

For example, when the corporate leaders of the city of Makati—known as the financial center of the Philippines, with the largest concentration of multinational and local corporations in the country—invited our firm to evaluate their highly urbanized district and provide recommendations to enhance their public image in the mid-2000s, some management team members assumed I'd come back with a proposal to build a big urban park or a grand, sweeping building. Instead, I returned with a list of twenty-one observations and recommendations, one of which was an obscure anomaly that no one noticed or would consider worthy of their time. But once we highlighted this small issue, it became one of the more important matters the leaders wanted to address regarding the perception of their city in the public eye.

During my daily walking treks through the Makati urban district, I kept noticing this small but curious anomaly: groups of maintenance crews applying a notable amount of hazard-yellow paint all over the place, from crosswalks and bollards to no-parking zones and curbs and loading docks, as well as other areas that the public came into contact with, including the base of high-profile buildings. While they intended to alert the public to potential hazards, they did their jobs too enthusiastically. The overabundance of this attention-grabbing yellow paint sent out the wrong signals of danger, fear, and threats while the district tried to entice corporate relocations, business investments, and residential purchases in the area. Although the leadership team had never noticed this anomaly, it was particularly glaring when I showed them photos of their city compared to the near absence of hazard-yellow paint in their competitor districts and developments. Like a movie with a few ill-suited prop selections that ruin a scene, noticing these anomalies and getting these small but concerning details under control is key to the successful experience of a place, whether it be a city, store, or institutional facility.

FIELD 3: COMPETITOR RECONNAISSANCE

We spend significant time studying our clients' competitors and kick-start the process by asking the same questions as above but with more of an indirect approach.

As part of this investigation, we learn as much as possible about the competitors' backgrounds, origin stories, strategic evolutions, experiments and misfires, and hints regarding their future directions. But since we don't have the luxury of interviewing these competitors directly, we conduct extensive research on our own and interview as many customers and tangential experts in the field as possible who can offer further insights about how a competitor operates and where they might head next.

A competitor's success can overwhelm some clients and intimidate them for their lack of perceived weakness. But instead of looking for a weakness or vulnerability in their competitors' armor, we recommend looking for a weakness in the customer/brand relationship, which we call "consumer indecision points."

No matter how great a brand might appear, each one has aspects where even the most loyal customers question their relationships, such as buying into Apple's mandatory ecosystem, Whole Foods' initial premium pricing and lack of Diet Coke and Doritos, or Trader Joe's limited assortment and chronically undersized parking lots.

By the end of this competitive analysis process, we're usually able to put together a solid picture of how the competitor thinks and operates, who their best customers are versus the ones on the fence, and where the most vulnerable "indecision points" exist in the customer/brand relationship.

FIELD 4: BACKGROUND EXPLORATIONS ON THE EDGES OF THE INDUSTRY

In every industry arena, the field is made up of the average players as well as the market leaders everyone knows about, studies, and follows. Chasing these leaders with a "me-too strategy" is a trap to put your brand in the crosshairs of an open battlefield. As Sam Walton, the founder of Walmart, once remarked, "If you want to beat me, don't try to copy me." Despite Walton's words ringing true for many leaders, many companies can't stop themselves from imitating the market leaders' strengths, which only flatters their competitors' position and dilutes their own brand's uniqueness.

Instead of chasing the market leaders, we recommend looking into the background of the industry to see what the smaller, nontraditional players are doing. We typically find these entities experimenting with big ideas and making moves that nobody notices, cares about, or worries will affect them. We identify, study, and keep close tabs on these outliers as they often contain kernels of golden insights into where society and customers are heading and what frustrating problems they wish brands could solve.

What most successful companies fail to realize is the historical pattern of how disruptions typically come from the background players in slow, clumsy ways. Such was the case when a small enterprise known as Netflix was trying to come up with a new way to satisfy customers' unmet needs that existed within the entertainment universe that Blockbuster pioneered and dominated. While Netflix's experimentations with mail-order DVDs and streaming hid in plain sight, their strategy seemed naive and unrealistic, yet yielded tremendous insights into where the entertainment industry could head next. However, the market leader, Blockbuster, wasn't paying attention to the background as much as they were eking out every bit of growth and profit in the foreground of their industry. The former CEO of Blockbuster, John Antioco, went as far as to say, "Netflix is destined to remain a very small niche business."

Netflix's eventual incursions into Blockbuster's brand fortress happen in varying degrees in every industry, whether Facebook to MySpace, SpaceX to Boeing, Chipotle to Taco Bell, Lululemon to Nike, or The Honest Company to the CPG companies. Instead of dismissing these small background players as idealistic startups and inconsequential players because of their low market share, we recommend learning as much as possible from their strategic maneuvers, experiments, and theories on where they believe the market is heading. Even if they don't end up redefining a sector, studying what opportunities they see emerging can sharpen your own future vision.

FIELD 5: CULTURAL CONVERSATIONS

One area that companies overlook is the imperceptible movements taking shape within society that may not be visible or apparent yet. A good consultant in touch with the culture and fashion of the times can help organizations get to the root of those movements and assess their potential impact on a client's industry and business.

Because of our intense focus and involvement in the restaurant industry, our firm was tracking the seemingly obscure "foodie" movement shortly after we opened our doors in the 1990s. Although we didn't hear the term used much in the mainstream, it reached a tipping point in the early 2000s, and our most progressive restaurant and food retailer clients were desperately trying to get this "foodie" merit badge and adapt their venues and brands to meet the tremendous growth potential this virtuous distinction afforded them. It was hard to say how big or how long the "foodie" movement would go on, but we knew there was something to it that could help our clients get ahead of it instead of having to chase it later. While some recognized and connected with the meaning and power of this word sooner than others, there were still many old-school holdouts in the food world that were late to the game. They frequently complained that their customers were asking too many questions about where their food came from and how it was produced and wondered why they were taking pictures of it, which seemed rude to some but was indicative of a cultural change. Today, we consider all those questions and pictures about food normal activities for the generation of millennials that have pushed the premiumization and gourmetization of food into the mainstream as the new baseline for "average" purchases, which boggles the mind of some older generations. But this tendency to trade up is a standard part of all generations' quest to live and eat better than their parents did. This fits in well with the larger tapestry of cultural food movements that have gained momentum over the last few decades, such as slow food, local food, organic food, fair-trade food, and even ethical dog food.

When this foodie movement began to emerge, the market opportunity to appeal to this obscure group of consumers seemed small and insignificant for the big, established industry players to bother with. But those companies that could see, detect, and decode the long-term impact of these movements—such as Whole Foods and Trader Joe's—had a tremendous advantage, if not jump, on the market growth opportunity that took other mainstream players fifteen years to catch up to.

Far too many retail leaders are not in touch with the culture or the fashion of the times. Because of their intense focus on hiring managers with strong logistics, data, and financial backgrounds, they're often missing the "feelers" in their organization who know how to read the tea leaves of society and keep up with how things are changing in culture.

Recently, an executive of a leading national grocery store chain commissioned our firm to help them develop a new prototype project in a progressive metro market. When I asked why they called us specifically, he said, "We don't understand food!" I found this statement both ironic and concerning since they were technically in the food business and had occupied a sizable role in the food industry for close to a hundred years.

When my team and I arrived to tour their stores, the vice president was excited to show us the prepared food department, where they displayed an indistinguishable mashing of Chinese, Japanese, Korean, and Thai food, all under the inappropriate banner of "Oriental Food." It'd be one thing if their stores were in remote, rural areas, but they were in progressive markets with diverse populations. Yet their leadership team was so out of touch with culture that it made us wonder if they "deserved" the business they sought. However, we bit our tongues and spent the next few weeks traveling the country and studying progressive food concepts and bringing them up to speed for why, where, and how food is changing in America before developing an international food hall concept that is now the envy of their market.

YOUR OUTPUT HINGES ON YOUR INPUTS

While conducting management interviews, on-site observations, competitor reconnaissance, background explorations, and cultural conversations sounds like a lot to do initially, the more a management team practices this multi-pronged approach, the more the comprehensive system becomes second nature. More importantly, approaching an innovation effort from as many different angles and frameworks as possible can lead to potential breakthroughs.

We can typically complete this part of our assignment within four to six weeks. But the most important thing we ask from everyone on the team is to turn off their instincts to "fix" and "solve" things—which is much harder than it sounds. Instead, we ask that they approach this phase with a nonjudgmental mindset of first just observing behavior and noticing small anomalies because that's where the golden nugget ideas reside.

Distill

"The model we choose to use to understand something determines what we find."

—Iain McGilchrist

THE DISTILL PHASE ENTAILS TAKING all the field notes, raw data, and observational insights we uncovered in the extract phase and placing them into specific categories—such as design, operations, or consumer behavior. This organization allows us the opportunity to examine them with more objective eyes in our lab.

Whenever there are people in places, things often appear chaotic or orderless on the surface. But with enough investigation, there's always an underlying logic and system for how things operate and how people behave in their environment. This phase aims to turn that disorder into clarity. We accomplish this through three techniques:

- "The Bucket List"
- "The Truth, the Lie, and the Positive Crisis"
- Our "Brand Dashboard," consisting of "solution," "meaning," and "experience" dials for each client

CREATE A BUCKET LIST

Regardless of the project size, we assemble a team of four to six professionals from a variety of disciplinary backgrounds like branding, advertising, graphic design, cultural anthropology, and architecture in order to study the behaviors, perceptions, and impressions of our client's place, products, organization, and customers.

We ask that each team member record observations without confirming, judging, or influencing each other's findings—at least not in the beginning two phases. Once we get back to headquarters, our team members summarize their observations of what they heard, saw, or felt happening in the field and interview room on index cards, again without influencing, biasing, or "correcting" each others' observations. We want to preserve that "first impression" quality and keep that initial perception intact because it usually contains more valuable insights than people realize. Though often unintentional, when the "experts" start correcting the "beginners" as to what they saw or heard, the most fruitful insights get cloaked in traditional disciplinary jargon or lost in siloed terminology, leading to more of the same industry recommendations.

It's not uncommon for us to find that the best architectural idea we get is from a branding expert or a cultural anthropologist. And sometimes, the best insight we get about cultural anthropology is from an architect or graphic designer. These findings speak to the importance of the beginner's mind, which we try to preserve for as long as possible.

Once we've amassed a pile of insight/anomaly/observation note cards on the war room table, we sort these findings into "buckets" with category headings like "design," "operations," "psychology," "branding," "industry," "format," "competitor," "culture," and so on. We then organize these buckets into a matrix of columns and rows on the wall to provide an overview of the scope of material we have to work with. Initially, our goal is to get the insights into the right category. Over the next several days, however, we'll start stacking the columns with the most insightful and pertinent ideas on top and work our way down.

DEFINE THE TRUTH, THE LIE, AND THE POSITIVE CRISIS

In addition to the buckets, we reserve the middle three columns for something we call "The Truth, the Lie, and the Positive Crisis."

The Lie

The Lie column is an intentionally exaggerated term we use to flag an issue we sense people are afraid to say out loud, but most everyone involved knows exists. In some organizations, this lie can come off as "The Emperor Has No Clothes." In others, it can be straight-up propaganda or boosterism. All organizations are guilty of possessing these unmentionable topics to varying degrees. Our purpose in highlighting them isn't to force the truth into the spotlight but to look for potential breakthroughs an unmentionable topic might reveal.

For instance, before Tesla's rise, we worked for an electric vehicle startup funded by big-name Wall Street investors and Washington power brokers. During our management interviews, we quickly sensed the tremendous pressure the executive team was under to have the first model of the car ready for a public launch date within a new retail format that had yet to be designed, much less located in a city. Like many investor-funded startups, things were moving at breakneck speed. Our primary concern was to protect our client from making a premature launch and embarrassing misfire.

While the battery technology was remarkably advanced, the vehicle's body styling, fit, and finish lagged way behind and wasn't ready for a public unveiling. We knew this, and so did the managers and department directors. Despite these concerns, the CEO declared that these issues didn't matter, and he didn't want anyone talking about them for fear of the issue leaking to anxious board members and nervous investors. It was risky for many inside and outside the organization to put their name and reputation behind this launch, yet nobody could discuss it openly.

We picked up on this issue and placed it in the Lie column in our office. While this column is confidential, my team and I looked at this statement daily until one day a solution hit us: Why don't we create a store concept that takes the car body off the vehicle to showcase the inner workings of electric vehicles? Even though this exposed approach to selling electric vehicles is more common today, it was a novel concept in the early 2000s. Most of the general public had no idea how electric cars worked, much less where the batteries were located in the vehicle. When we opened the store, this "inner-workings" approach created tremendous public interest and curiosity from electric vehicle enthusiasts and more traditionally-minded consumers who typically bought a car based on its styling, speed, power, status, and sex appeal, none of which this car had.

The car release was so successful that a major automobile manufacturer eventually bought the company, technology, and store showroom concept for a handsome sum because of the startup's battery technology and revolutionary retailing presentation.

The Truth

The Truth column may include comments or observations from customers, employees, outside experts, journalists, investors, or even our diverse staff that describe the situation accurately without trying to be polite or politically correct.

During a meeting with an influential board member of a large retail organization, we diplomatically discussed the poor condition of the 251 stores they'd built across the state. Although the stores were the worst-maintained facilities in the industry, I was careful not to offend this board member with such a fatal analysis in my opening remarks. However, she made our jobs easier when she blurted out, "The condition of our stores is murdering our brand!" Though the management team didn't want to hear this assessment, we put her comment straight into the Truth column and helped us identify a future crisis for the brand/customer relationship as we soon discovered a more progressive competitor had announced plans to come into the market with their shiny, new, state-of-the-art flagship stores. We knew we had to get this issue on the table, despite being an uncomfortable topic to discuss.

The Positive Crisis

The Positive Crisis column describes what happens to our client's brand and place of business if they do nothing but maintain the status quo. Understandably, many organizations get apprehensive about taking on bold new initiatives, and some don't want to put anything at risk, making innovation impossible. But it's important to consider that the cost of doing nothing also comes with substantial risk. To gain clarity, we try to get as specific as possible by asking questions like:

- "What if our client just keeps doing business as usual, using the existing systems, formats, and programs they already have in place?"

- "What would be the harm, financial cost, or impact of doing nothing?"

- "What would the consumer and competitor reaction be if they just stayed the course as currently configured and equipped?"

- "How long could our client's business remain open and profitable without investing in a new store format and experience?"

The honest answers to these questions can be quite revealing, if not alarming, which is precisely why we must bring them to light.

We don't always show clients the Truth or Lie column but use them more for internal purposes to get our bearings straight and identify potential issues. However, we keep the positive crisis front and center during every future client meeting. Why this emphasis? Because most organizations won't change unless they have to. As with any maturing organism, the older and more established the organization and brand is, the harder it will be to install a new way of thinking, doing business, or going to market, which is why we frequently remind management teams, "Learning is easy, but forgetting is the hard part."

Some executives don't want to talk about doom and gloom scenarios out of fear of eroding staff morale and sparking an exodus of employees and investors. And some politically-minded leaders won't even allow what they deem "negative talk"—what my team and I call "reality"—into their boardrooms and strategy discussions. They only want to hear about the good news and the positive opportunities. But the problem with only talking about "opportunities" is that it focuses on what would be nice to pursue someday but not what organizations must do to survive.

As worn out as the old cliché of "necessity is the mother of invention" is, no words could ring more true for motivating leaders to prioritize innovation over the usual analysis paralysis many aging companies find themselves saddled with. When a company believes it might die, the organization, like any organism, will fight like hell to survive. It will stop wishing and start focusing on the most urgent priorities, as nothing spurs action more than a clear and present danger. Therefore, we keep that positive crisis front and center in all our discussions so that the team members will develop the courage they need to make brave decisions.

INSTALL A BRAND DASHBOARD

While the buckets in the previous exercise help us understand how we look at consumer behavior, internal management issues, and external industry movements, these findings don't represent the perspective for how consumers look at, think about, or catalog our clients' place brand. Instead, we find that consumers make subconscious snap judgments about a place brand according to three general questions:

1. "What problem does your brand and store help me solve?"
2. "What additional layer of value or meaning do you provide for me beyond just the commodity aspects?"
3. "What kind of experience (i.e., work vs. pleasure) will I have if I go there?"

These three questions are paramount for organizations and their consultants to monitor, gauge, and adjust. Because this information is so vital for survival, we've created a "dashboard" tool for evaluating the health, clarity, and relevance of their place brand contract with the public consisting of three simple dials—solutions, meaning, and experience—that go from 1 (poor) to 10 (excellent).

#1 The Solutions Dial

Humans are a solution-seeking species. We wake up each day with a series of small, medium, and large problems to solve. Some of our small-level problems may entail deciding what to feed the kids for breakfast or what to wear to an important meeting, while our medium-level problems might include finding a new diet plan or investing strategy for retirement. Our larger-level problems, though, are harder to get our arms around. They may include things like finding a renewed sense of purpose now that the kids are out of the house, figuring out how to care for your aging mother-in-law who can't provide for herself, trying to deal with midlife depression, or finding meaning and hope after an unexpected death, divorce, or bankruptcy.

Some problems are functional, like, "I need to find a gas station quickly," while others are more emotional and aspirational, like, "I want to buy products from companies that support diversity or save the rainforest," or "I need to bring back the spark in my marriage."

In the old days, we traditionally looked to patriarchal and matriarchal figures such as the president, pastor, mayor, sheriff, local doctor, or school principal for guidance. But we no longer rely on or trust these authority positions and the institutions they represent as much as we did in the past. As the legendary business strategist and bestselling author Seth Godin states, "Our new civic and scientific and professional life, though, is all about doubt. About questioning the status quo, questioning marketing or political claims, and most of all, questioning what's next." For better or worse, we now look to brands like Nike, Pfizer, TED Talks, Merrill Lynch, WeightWatchers, and Goop to help solve problems and guide us on where to aim our lives.

But just like consumer brands (toothpaste, soap, cars, etc.), place brands need clarity on what problems their venues solve for customers. For instance, is your place about convenience, efficiency, indulgence, experience, community, art, adventure, or enlightenment? The more unique, proprietary, and compelling your benefits and solution to a consumer problem are, the more you'll be able to offer consumers something they can't find or replicate elsewhere. But you can't always ask consumers about their problems and expect them to describe them clearly. The most profound brands know what's wrong and what we need better than we know ourselves.

Getting extreme clarity on the problem your organization and place brand solves is essential in today's hypercompetitive environment. Despite this, it's not uncommon that my team and I find everyone in the organization—from the CEO to managers to the frontline employees—has a slightly different answer and perspective, which leads to brand dissonance and confusion internally and externally.

Your place brand's solution needs to be clear and consistent up and down the organizational ladder. Customers won't waste their time and energy trying to figure out how your place can help improve their lives. You only have a few seconds to grab customers' attention and get them interested and excited about the problem-solving capabilities of your place. If it takes too long to grasp or too much effort to figure out, customers move on to the next, more compelling option.

#2 The Meaning Dial

Humans are a meaning-seeking species. We need meaning to explain why the world is so harsh and unfair; why people get ill and die; why we age and lose our hair; why our eyes, knees, and hearts don't work as well as they used to; and why the world seems so uncertain and unstable at times. More than anything, we need meaning to guide us onto the right path to put our lives back in balance.

Many companies think "branding" is something you spray on top of a product or store like magic aerosol instead of making the meaning a core part of the product offering and experience. While many business-minded clients avoid this esoteric topic of meaning because they believe it's too fluffy, they do so at their own peril. Why? Because as online forces continue to commoditize everything, one of the few viable differentiating factors companies and institutions have left is to infuse their offering with meaning.

What do I mean by meaning? Pick your flavor: religionism, patriotism, workism, veganism, localism, nationalism, globalism, activism, spiritualism, and so on. Meaning originally came from tribal leaders, religious institutions, and government institutions. But today, we look to brands to provide us with meaning that can give us explanations, ideas, inspirations, and solutions for how to live better.

In our work for Whole Foods, we uncovered the powerful belief and meaning that "Mother Earth knows better than the chemistry labs at Big Food conglomerates." And in working with Harley-Davidson, we tapped into the rich meaning that the brand uniquely contains around the universal ideas of freedom, rebellion, and "sticking it to the man."

Meaning is one of the most important yet challenging qualities to define. But that's the mission most companies, institutions, and place brands need to figure out before putting together a set of blueprints for their place.

This is where creating a "Field of Meaning," which we discussed in chapter six, consisting of cultural reference points, artifacts, icons, and symbols that relate to your company's values, beliefs, and aspirations, comes into play. These symbols might include cultural references like an eagle (patriotism: Harley-Davidson), a farmer using a sickle in the field (agrarianism: Whole Foods), or a tractor (Harvest Market) inside the produce section of a grocery store.

Once you discover a robust Field of Meaning that you can associate and tie to your brand, you can drill down into why these values, beliefs, legends, stories, mythologies, and symbols mean something to the people you want to attract. If you seek the fastest, lightest, cheapest, and most easy to finance motorcycle on the market, buying a Harley is probably not for you as this isn't what the brand stands for. But after experiencing an ugly divorce or quitting a dead-end career, you might find riding on the road with a bunch of Harley fanatics to the Sturgis Rally incredibly therapeutic, bonding, or even life-changing.

The key is to uncover what you and your brand care about and what you're willing to fight for to preserve, protect, or defend. Within that territory is where your brand values and beliefs reside, and the next pivotal question to uncover is how many other people feel the same way and are passionate about the same issues.

#3 The Experience Dial

Humans are an experience-seeking species. We need sensory activation, experiential stimulation, and social engagement to keep our minds sharp.

For example, during the pandemic, many of us felt a sense of social isolation and a lack of sensory activation. This detachment from the world can lead to a host of other cognitive impairment concerns such as fatigue, stress, poor quality sleep, inability to concentrate and remember things, and even depression among populations of people who never previously had psychological issues. Socializing with others can enhance memory, prevent dementia, and improve concentration. But the pandemic shut down most of our regular encounters with the grocery store cashier, coffee shop barista, restaurant waiter, barber, and bartender. It also prevented us from hanging out with our friends, neighbors, coworkers, and extended family members. Something as simple as talking to somebody on the bus or train ride back home can make our day more interactive. Instead, most of us had one long work-from-home blur of indistinguishable days, which over extended periods can lead to undifferentiated memories.

We catalog and differentiate our memories by remembering where we were when the memory happened. But if the place where we made that memory is the same place we experience every day, it can make our memories less definable, distinctive, and differentiated.

As described in chapter three, most of the ideas we have in our heads and most of the language we use comes from a sensory-based understanding, modeling, and memory of the world. The more a brand can help people activate their senses, the more memorable and sticky it will be in their brains. Ideally, you want to stimulate the customers' sensory organs in the real world, but you can also activate people's senses through movies, songs, and other art forms. While an engaging film might be fake, it can still make us laugh, scream, and cry actual tears in a room full of strangers, and so can the right kind of atmospheric stimuli and immersive experiences.

The experience dial is the most common dimension designers focus on, but they tend to do that more on a conscious, intellectual level than a subconscious, sensory level. I frequently encounter place brands with only the experience dial engaged, without having any discernable connection to or development of the solutions and meaning dials, which leaves their customers confused and their brands vulnerable to competitive threats.

PUTTING THE DIALS INTO PRACTICE

Once organizations install this dashboard of dials, they inevitably have questions. Below are my recommendations for the most common ones I get asked.

Which Dial Should We Start With First?

I recommend clients develop their place brand strategy by starting with the solutions dial first and the meaning dial second. The experience dial should be last in the process as it manifests the solutions and meanings in tangible form and shape. A visitor to a place should be able to grasp the solution and feel the meaning of the place viscerally, without much work or mental calculus.

We only have a few seconds to convey this solution/meaning feeling to consumers through brand touchpoints and experiential cues and triggers. Thus, these icons, symbols, surrogates, hieroglyphics, and cultural references must come preloaded with psychological meaning, cultural content, and latent emotional potential. Everything communicates, and like a good movie director, you're trying to set the scene just right to tell your brand's story and invite your customers on a worthwhile quest.

Does It Matter If Each of the Dials Says Something Different?

No matter how you slice it, great brands like Apple, Starbucks, and Nike always express the same core idea, message, and feeling in their stores, packaging, customer service, and advertising messages. This consistency is due to how closely they align—and reinforce—their brand's solution, meaning, and experience, which creates a compelling compounding effect and undeniable emotional coherency.

Yet, we find many place brands with contradictory messages and signals in these three dials. Their advertising message says "high quality," while the store experience says "cheap, rock-bottom pricing." Like a tuning fork, consumers subconsciously notice when brands strike harmonious tones and emotional vibes with them versus those that are hard to make sense of and feel disharmonious.

For instance, Whole Foods pioneered one of the most robust Fields of Meaning we'd ever seen in the grocery industry. They created a culture, cause, and tribe of loyal followers willing to advocate, evangelize, and defend the brand. I have nothing but admiration and awe for the groundbreaking vision that John Mackey, one of the founders of Whole Foods, brought to the grocery industry. His genuine concern for where good food comes from and its effect on our health and environment was so desperately needed and unconventional for its time that the established corporate chains didn't know how to compete, much less catch up to Whole Foods. He is not without his controversies, but creating a cultural movement requires an eccentric viewpoint and entails ruffling some feathers along the way. Since Amazon acquired Whole Foods in 2017 for $13.6 billion, that robust Field of Meaning has been watered down. The solution has become more about price and deals (which many other grocery stores already own perceptually), making the experience feel even more expensive because of the lack of meaning. Although it could've become one of the biggest cult brands of our era, many consumers consider Whole Foods just another ordinary mass-market grocery store, which is not only a shame but a missed opportunity.

The special halo Whole Foods created justified its premium, but without a robust Field of Meaning, it will face increasing pressure to treat its product offerings as commodities. Worse yet, Whole Foods's decrease in meaning has created a sizable opening for new players to take over the mantle of becoming the premier store for those customers passionate about the healthy, organic, and natural food movement, which continues its evolution into new territories.

How Can We Monitor Our Performance on Each of the Dials?

Once a company embarks on creating a place brand dashboard, we recommend evaluating the health and performance of each dial on a scale of 1–10 annually, if not quarterly or monthly, but not every decade, as is common practice. To get started, we recommend regularly asking customers and employees these questions:

- Why would you consider using our brand? (solution)
- When you think of our brand, what comes to mind? (meaning)
- When you're around our brand environment, do you feel comfortable, anxious, beautiful, poor, inspired? (experience)

Is It Okay If We Lean on One Dial More Than the Others?

Most companies have a higher degree of talent, passion, and performance for one dial, with a decreasing strength in the other two dials. This predisposition to lean on one dial is normal, but you can't afford to ignore your weaker dials, as they can hurt you down the road. While being famous for one dial is okay, I recommend bringing all dials to a competent level (7–8 out of 10). This minimum will allow you to stay relevant and integrated with the ever-shifting playing field of your particular industry and to fend off competitors exploiting vulnerable "indecision points." The homework assignment for most organizations is to keep improving the weaker dials.

How Long Does It Take to Change the Perception of a Brand?

Taking a brand to the next level of excellence is less like a microwave and more like a slow cooker. It takes time for new brand initiatives to simmer in the market and for customers to notice the enhanced flavors. But the more sticky and memorable a new place brand experience is, the more likely it is to dislodge the old brand taste and replace it with a new, more favorable one. For this reason, we recommend exaggerating design gestures in critical areas and around key values.

The older a brand is, the more ingrained the image, memory, and experience becomes inside consumers' minds. However, we can typically change the image of a place within a one-to-three-year time frame, depending on the level of investment in their brand experience. The key is getting the brand clarified, expressed, and manifested to a Level 10 for all three dials.

Articulate

"Everything should be made as simple as possible, but not simpler."

—Albert Einstein

THE ARTICULATION PHASE SYNTHESIZES OUR best insights and ideas into a coherent strategy and game plan that builds consensus with the organizational leaders and inspires them to take action with a sense of urgency and conviction.

Our goal is to get as simple and profound as possible. But achieving this profound simplicity requires combing through our ideas and detangling the knots. To expedite this process, we use a series of exercises and techniques—an innovation tool kit—to turn our patchwork of ideas into a strategic game plan. This tool kit includes the following exercises:

- Developing a "theory on the market"
- Creating an "internal tagline"

- "Finding the funny".
- Pursuing a "seemingly impossible idea"
- Determining who consumers "become" when they enter a venue
- Codifying a "brand constitution"
- Zeroing in on the "six tips of the brand spear" for each of our clients

DEVELOP A "THEORY ON THE MARKET"

Although "innovation" is the buzzword of our era, the business culture focuses heavily on error reduction and efficiency metrics. Perhaps it's the imprint of the Henry Ford assembly line or the increasing commoditization of nearly everything. But true innovation is the opposite of error reduction and chasing efficiency metrics. It's about making as many mistakes as possible in rapid succession and putting profit and efficiency standards at risk by venturing into the dark, uncharted territories of an industry.

Even though companies tend to be very good at analyzing what their problems are and where the errors exist in their operation, they often don't have the appetite or stomach for making bets on the future. This reluctance is understandable, considering the scrutiny of investors and how bonuses and promotions within organizations reward efficiencies and penalize those who make mistakes. But creating an innovation culture is about allowing individuals to experiment, be inefficient, and make mistakes without career-ending penalties. It's about teaching managers to place well-studied and calculated bets on where they think consumers will head next.

Scouting where new and emerging market opportunities reside can make or break a company's future success and leadership potential. But instead of betting wildly, we help our clients develop a provocative and compelling "theory on the market" for where they believe things will head for their business, industry, and customers. Experience has shown us that those great ideas and perspectives usually exist buried within managers, and it's our job to help surface, fortify, and outfit them with the right equipment to survive the scrutiny of the "efficiency police" and committee hearings.

A company without a theory on the market is a sign of trouble ahead because if you don't have a strong opinion on where your industry and the consumers are heading, it begs whether you deserve to grow your business. Consumers are never satisfied with what they already have—sweaters, cars, shoes, food, and TV shows—and always want to hear about the next new thing. As a result, brands must constantly be serving up platters of what customers will need and want next.

To articulate where your industry is heading, I recommend our clients start by asking two pivotal questions:

- Which unmet need do your customers possess but don't yet know they're missing?
- If you suddenly got hired by your fiercest competitor and were now sitting at their strategy table, how would you recommend they beat your old employer?

The more provocative and daring your theory is, the better. People today don't get excited about average. They want to follow brands and places that break new ground and take them to new and exciting places. Practice putting your theory out there in written and verbal form to everyone you meet, like a comedian would when ironing out and perfecting a new joke. Keep chiseling and honing the pitch down to a sharp point until it creates an "aha" moment for your internal teams and external audiences. And, of course, continue testing and refining it.

CREATE AN "INTERNAL TAGLINE"

In the groundbreaking book *The Attention Merchants*, author Tim Wu describes a fascinating conversation that took place at New York's Plaza Hotel in 1966 between two controversial yet game-changing academics: the recently fired Harvard psychology professor, pioneering philosopher, and advocate of psychedelic drugs Timothy Leary and media theorist Marshall McLuhan.

Although Leary was a rising star in the counterculture world, he was concerned, if not repulsed, by advertising's impact on society and his generation's perspective. He sought McLuhan's advice on how to "reach all the disaffected" in a world full of corporate branding motives and advertising agendas. Instead of running away from advertising, McLuhan suggested he embrace the approach and use the advertising techniques himself. In other words: fight fire with fire. That conversation eventually led Leary and his cohorts to come up with the profoundly simple but generation-defining tagline, "Turn on, Tune in, Drop out." This phrase perfectly captured the mood of the counterculture and defined the spirit of that particular generation's intent to remake society in their own view, which they did in spades.

Coming up with a tagline that grabs people's attention, stokes their emotions, and compels them to take action isn't easy. But it's a super effective way to capture the brilliance of an idea or movement in a few short words. Although clients regularly hire our firm to develop taglines for their brands and marketing campaigns, we also believe in creating an "internal tagline" to help guide our internal thinking and express the essence of our idea early in the strategy process.

Our process for materializing a profoundly simple tagline requires patience. In the beginning stages of a strategic exploration, it might take us ten thousand words (about one hour) to get our clumsy, inelegant thoughts out onto the table, and some management teams can't handle this messiness. But by working with the client in an iterative process, we'll chisel those words down to five thousand by the next board update, then one thousand, then fifty, all the way down to five or fewer piercing words.

To kick-start this process, my team and I use the technique of communicating our big strategic idea in the tight confines and limits of a movie poster. Using a pop-culture frame of reference like this helps us focus on the most compelling imagery and a few short words to provoke immediate interest and illustrate our idea to anyone from grandparents to their teenage grandchildren.

The movie poster's job is to present a compelling story and journey worth taking in short, accessible terms that inspire audiences enough to buy a ticket. Taglines such as "Who you gonna call?" for *Ghostbusters* or "Just when you thought it was safe to go back in the water" for *Jaws 2*, or "Everyone wants to be found" for *Lost in Translation* got audiences off the couch and into the movie theater in droves.

But if a movie poster isn't clear, concise, and persuasive enough, audience members are unlikely to pay the price of admission to see it, and producers won't fund it. The same applies to getting studio executives to commit the time, money, and resources to move forward with an ambitious innovation effort.

While I'm not suggesting you create an actual movie poster or public tagline at this early point in the strategy development process, I do recommend creating an internal tagline to help summarize the strategic value proposition of your place into a sharp, piercing catchphrase that can provide immediate interest and enlightenment to entice leaders to get on board with it.

The beauty of conducting this tagline exercise is that it forces us to capture the essence, quest, and magic of a place in a few short, piercing words and then challenges us to come up with creative ways to visualize them through seductive design imagery.

Below are a few examples of internal taglines we've developed for clients, some of which eventually became public taglines.

- **"Nature's on our side."** People seeking an island resort vacation typically head there for the "sun and sand." But our famous Hawaiian island resort client had a perennial problem: their side of the island is one of the top ten wettest places on Earth. Their annual marketing plan was to pray it doesn't rain much. Our solution: turn the negative of rain into a positive connection to experience nature and feel its transformative ability to cleanse the soul.

- **"Work Hard. Ride Hard."** When your brand is the archetype of freedom, rebellion, and "sticking it to the man," it can be hard to be the "boss" (the man) and expect younger employees to abide by the rules. Our solution for Scott Fischer Enterprises—the premier founder of many successful Harley-Davidson dealerships across the U.S.—was to remind employees of the secret to success: working hard, then playing hard. In that order. Although this was an internal tagline, customers also loved it because they saw their work/riding lives from the same perspective.

- **"Close to home."** A national steak buffet chain struggles with the commoditization of its industry and the relentless pressure to compete solely on price. They make a better product but don't get credit for it. Our solution: build an environment and experience that reminds customers that their place and food is about as close to home as it gets to homestyle cooking.

- **"A healthy indulgence."** During the meteoric rise of Whole Foods in the early 2000s, there was increasing pressure to expand the offering to appeal to broader audiences, and many heated internal management debates ensued about what should or shouldn't be allowed on the shelves. There were no easy answers, but we found the debate of tremendous value in and of itself. Our solution: embrace the tension and help customers have their cake and eat their kale, too, by becoming the experts in offering a healthy indulgence that feels natural and doesn't make you feel guilty.

- **"Everyone's Downtown."** A well-known public outdoor pedestrian mall in Santa Monica, California, encounters strong headwinds as it competes with private mall developers with much larger budgets. The public district becomes overidentified as a place for tourists while losing its "cool" with locals. Our solution: shift from the pedestrian mall image to its real downtown roots and remind the public that it's not an elitist, exclusive, or a private place but everyone's downtown.

- **"Bring your table to life."** An Oklahoma grocery store chain faces increasing pressure from national chains. They can't win on price, variety, or convenience, nor do they have a strong point of view about their offering. Our solution: focus on what people in the local community care about and devote much of their free time and money to doing: spending quality time with their families and friends around the iconic symbol of the table in all forms (kitchen table, dining room tables, patio tables, picnic tables, etc.) and offer them delicious and inspiring ways to bring their family's tables to life.

- **"Handle with Care."** As described in chapter two, the Alberta grocery store chain Freson Bros. also faced intense pressure from the retail giants and tech disruptors to compete on price, variety, and convenience. But they possessed a strong set of values, a belief in treating everyone like family, and a passion for honoring the traditions of food that needed capturing in words and experience. Our solution: focus on the little things that make a big difference in customers' lives, such as respecting the craft of food and making the extra effort to handle everything in the store with care.

I use this tagline exercise in all areas of my business and personal life. In the early stages of writing this book, I forced myself to go through the tagline exercise and came up with the internal title *Irreplaceable: Saving Humanity One Place at a Time.* Even though I didn't ultimately use this subtitle, the exercise helped me capture and clarify the book's essence in a few short words.

Many intellectuals dismiss the tagline exercise as "cute." However, when they try it themselves and see how challenging it is to boil their strategy down into one compelling idea, they recognize its value.

FIND THE FUNNY

Whenever my team and I take on a new project assignment, we initially have a thousand "brilliant" ideas for what our clients need to do to move their business forward. But the deeper we venture out into the dark swamps of the assignment, the more we find ourselves lost and creatively stuck in the mud, unsure of which direction to head next. This feeling of being lost can create panic in creatives and cause many sleepless nights, particularly when there's a deadline looming. When this happens, I remind my staff that pulling our hair out is exactly where we need to be for the big ideas to break free.

The key to getting unstuck is seeing the same problem from another angle, and one exercise that consistently helps us achieve this is to "find the funny" in the situation.

In our innovation work for Harley-Davidson, a brand we revere and consider almost a religion, we found ourselves stuck in the middle of a big assignment. Our internal brainstorming meetings grew tense as our deadline for presenting to the executive leadership team counted down quickly while the pressure to perform in the big leagues of brand dynasties ratcheted up. Part of the stress came from reading all the in-depth studies and reports about how the metric bikes from Europe and Asia were faster, lighter, cheaper, and winning all the races in various categories. As I looked through our research photos and reviewed my interview notes with folks like Ernie, who I referenced at the beginning of this book, I joked with my team out of dire frustration that they should've titled our assignment "How to sell the slowest, fattest, most expensive, and hardest to finance motorcycle on the market to midlife crisis males fading in strength." It was just an offhand joke that got everyone laughing, but then we all recognized the genius of the statement as light bulbs went off in our heads.

Selling a fast, cheap bike has its place in the minds of some consumers. But solving the end of loneliness for a particular life stage that all consumers eventually face speaks to a much broader and more compelling experience value proposition that many consumers would be willing to crawl through mud to acquire. And with that spark, our creative momentum hit top speed.

Instead of putting the bike on the pedestal like many Harley dealerships had been doing for years in stores, we focused on putting the community—and, therefore, the end of loneliness—front and center as our leading value proposition. To accomplish this, we brainstormed creating actual bonfires outside the stores to encourage people to hang out and designing community areas inside the store that brought people who had never met before together. We developed plans to turn the humdrum "Maytag Repairman" parts counter into a lively "parts bar" with stools and countertops like a real bar. We turned the parts department person into a "parts-tender" whose role was similar to a bartender, which isn't just to serve drinks but to serve as a social facilitator to foster customer connections and make everyone feel like they belong (think *Cheers* meets *Sons of Anarchy* clubhouse). Rather than discouraging customers from hanging out in the stores, we created a clubhouse and fort-like atmosphere for those customers who feel disenfranchised from so many other parts of retail society, like hipster coffee shops or luxury yoga studios. While the target Harley customers may not have felt like they fit in a Blue Bottle Coffee shop or SoulCycle sweat box, we zeroed in on making them the main star and hero of the Harley store and story.

When we presented this concept to the Harley executives, we were nervous about how they would take it, but as the legendary story consultant and author Robert McKee says about comedy, "Laughter settles all arguments." We know from experience that if we can get serious business leaders laughing, we've hit upon an undeniable human truth. But just like the challenge of any comedian, the first half of the joke terrified them (and us) as it came out of our mouth—"How to sell the slowest, fattest . . ."—but the punch line of the "end of loneliness" had them involuntarily laughing because the truth of the joke is unmistakable, although intentionally exaggerated. From there, we agreed to build stores with a greater focus on helping potential customers realize that buying a Harley came with more than just a new set of wheels but also included thousands of friends and a tight-knit community that made you feel like you belong to something much bigger than yourself.

We've used this "find the funny" approach in every project we've worked on and have hundreds of stories about the truth of our clients' businesses and their customers' habits and behaviors in the stores. The best jokes we hear come from listening to employees or customers speaking "off the record" as they say something they'd never tell their bosses or report in a formal survey. This extraction technique is about the art of conversation. It's about listening and getting the people you interview so comfortable and relaxed that they'll tell you anything and say things without trying to be diplomatic or professional, much like how friends converse when talking with each other over a drink. Those truths are the raw gold we're after, but they can be near impossible to surface in formal interviews, business settings, or survey questions. It's like asking your friend what they thought of *Mission: Impossible* versus being asked by a movie critic or college English professor. I'm more interested in the casual friend's response than the expert's formal interpretation.

You'd be amazed by how many hilarious human truths there are to laugh about in watching people engage with buildings, shop for products, and interact with others. And there's a reason workplace sitcoms like *The Office*, *Cheers*, and *Superstore* tickle viewers' funny bones and have been a celebrated genre for decades. If you look at these human interactions from the right angle, there's a lot of good material to use for innovation.

My advice to clients and consultants is to find the funny in your business and be willing to laugh at yourself. It may just serve as the critical thread that helps you spin the next big innovation—while enjoying some laughter along the way.

EMBRACE YOUR "SEEMINGLY IMPOSSIBLE" IDEAS

Every day my team and I work in industries that require extensive knowledge, training, and expertise to run, which we don't have. But fortunately, we don't have to be experts in our clients' businesses or industries to uncover big insights or develop breakthrough concepts. If anything, that would hurt our beginner's minds and limit our creativity. We just need to be experts at the process of decoding human behaviors, identifying the rules for how an industry competes, and distilling those factors down into a set of dials and instruments we can fiddle with and adjust until we hit the right frequency.

Most industry life cycles start wild, disorganized, and misaligned in the beginning stages. Assuming the players in that field have a great product, they can charge higher prices and make many mistakes without severe penalties. But as industries evolve and mature, they operate according to an implicit set of rules and boundaries established by professional trade associations, the regulatory environment, industry standards, competitor actions, and customer expectations. These market forces eventually push the players into a more defined and comparable set of offerings, prices, features, and benefits. And with or without meaning it, the players on the field eventually embrace and adapt to the same best practices, standards, and proven techniques. Over time, the various companies that make up an industry begin to look alike and offer similar value propositions, which frequently happens in consumer categories like hotels, computers, cars, airlines, groceries, and cell phones. Once this industry alignment takes hold, companies face the threat of becoming a common commodity and have to consider one of two options: maxing out efficiency gains to lower costs and prices or adding more features and benefits to their value proposition and more dollars to their marketing budgets.

Both options can provide noticeable gains in the short term, but both approaches will eventually reach their upper limits of dividends, making it harder and harder to impress customers and stand out in the long run. If customers don't notice a meaningful enough difference within a competitive set, the cheaper option will always win.

While maximizing efficiency gains, cutting costs, lowering prices, and adding more features that benefit customers, it doesn't always benefit companies. That might sound illogical. But making better, cheaper, more convenient products and services in mature industries often leads to a "buyer's market" with diminishing returns for the sellers.

Companies can overcome this competitive stalemate by constantly seeking new and emerging markets where the profits are better and the customer/ competitor terms less intense and more forgiving. But how do you find these fertile markets? By jumping over the industry's fences to explore the "seemingly impossible" ideas that no one has dared to pursue. The key to business innovation is continually exploring, investigating, and experimenting with these seemingly impossible ideas. Why? Because this territory is where:

- Latent opportunities lie waiting to be activated

- Competitors are reluctant to venture into

- Future industry disruptions will most likely occur

Many corporate leaders won't tolerate discussing these seemingly impossible ideas because they assume the exploration process is a dead-end road that wastes time, energy, and resources. But for those executives with the vision, courage, and fortitude to venture beyond industry borders, it can mean the difference between leading the market instead of always following it.

One of our more courageous clients, Niemann Foods, owns and operates over one hundred supermarkets, pharmacies, convenience, pet, and hardware stores in Illinois, Indiana, Iowa, and Missouri. While most organizations of this size would focus their investments in the brands they already have in motion, the astute CEO of that organization, Rich Niemann, sensed the

changes in the grocery industry with the retail giants and tech disruptors infiltrating his territory and wanted to explore the possibility of creating a more
bold and progressive grocery store concept to add to his stable of brands. But
instead of chasing the market leaders' focus on price, size, and variety, we
worked with Rich and his team to develop a new brand/prototype concept
that tapped into his passion for ranching. We designed an entirely new store
concept built off an existing, underleveraged name he had in his stable called
Harvest Market.

Listening to Rich talk about ranching, cattle, crops, tractors, and the daily
struggles small family farms endure got us fired up and allowed us to create a fertile "Field of Meaning" to build a brand position, platform, and food
philosophy. Rich and his team were on board with the brand strategy and
concept from the get-go. But what motivated these leaders the most was when
we presented our "Seemingly Impossible" idea of developing a real-life butter
churning station inside their store where they could craft farm-fresh butter the
way farmers made it in a multitude of butter-log flavors such as honey, chive,
and herb. This animated station is a big feature of the store and goes a long way
to demonstrate to customers how they can taste the "farm difference" of the
Harvest Market brand.

The new Harvest Market prototype stores are a massive hit with the public
and have won many industry awards. Future iterations of this prototype will
continue to push the boundaries of what a grocery store can achieve by taking
on more seemingly impossible ideas.

HELP CUSTOMERS BECOME SOMEONE ELSE

Most of us have titles attached to our lives, such as mom, dad, boss, manager, employee, student, and loyal son or daughter. While these labels come
with benefits and responsibilities, they rarely represent the full picture of who
we truly are, as there are always other sides of ourselves we'd like to explore,
indulge in, and even dream about someday becoming.

One of the ways we get in touch with our other personas is by going to
places that help us explore those other sides. For instance, the person I am at

my client's sleek skyscraper offices in Manhattan differs from the relaxed, fun guy I become on game day when my two cheesehead friends drag me to see the Green Bay Packers play at Lambeau Field. What I wear, eat and drink, and how I talk and behave changes based on my environment. The person I am at work versus the person I am at a vacation resort in the Caribbean couldn't be further apart. But I can't just make these mental shifts alone; I need the right environment and props to help facilitate my other personas and get me in the perfect mood. And like a skillful movie director, I need a talented design team to help transport me to another place and state of mind.

As Alain de Botton describes so eloquently in his book *The Architecture of Happiness*, "Belief in the significance of architecture is premised on the notion that we are, for better or worse, different people in different places—and on the conviction that it is architecture's task to render vivid to us who we might ideally be."

Whenever my team and I are working on a project, we spend a considerable amount of time putting ourselves in the shoes of the ideal occupants of the space while asking three pivotal questions:

1. **Who do I become while here?**
   If I go through the effort to visit your place, will I appear more intelligent, classy, sexy, rugged, revered, or hard to resist? Will I become more powerful, empowered, skilled, or informed? Or will I feel more energized, relaxed, enlightened, or cultured? To be more specific, will I become a polo player (Ralph Lauren store), a badass (Harley-Davidson), an aristocrat (Rolls-Royce dealership), a great parent (Disneyland), a spiritually minded person (religious facility), or a high-rolling big shot (Las Vegas) who lives by the creed "What happens in Vegas, stays in Vegas"?

2. **How will your place transform me?**
   The secret to understanding humans is to realize we constantly seek "state changes." We want to go from fat to thin, poor to rich, dirty to clean, stressed to relaxed, tasteless to tasteful, unhealthy to healthy, lonely to popular, old to young, good to great, and weak to strong. But

we can't do these things alone; we need people, products, and places to serve as catalysts and agents of change to help get us there. So the question place-makers and managers must clarify is "What will happen to me if I go there?" And "How will I be changed, enhanced, improved, or bettered by visiting this place?"

3. **How will I know how to act?**

    We all know how to act and behave in a library versus a sports bar because we can read the signals and props of the room. But without those pivotal cues and triggers, we risk wearing the wrong clothes and projecting the wrong image, attitude, and mindset.

    As mentioned, everything communicates—carpets, columns, doorknobs, bedsheets, pavers, sounds, aromas, paint colors, and so on. Place-makers and place-managers must recognize the signals their places transmit to guests. And they must be intentional about and coordinate these signs and symbols with all the other brand components from the Field of Meaning.

When my team and I are developing the brand strategy and design of a place, we keep these questions at the forefront of our thinking just as a movie director would do to ensure they transmit the right ideas and elicit the specific emotions and perceptions from the audience. But we frequently encounter places that aren't empathetic to the consumer's feelings and impose the designer's or starchitect's ego on the audience members, preventing them from relating or connecting with the content on a personal level.

CODIFY YOUR PLACE BRAND CONSTITUTION

Organizations have to make countless decisions regarding brand names, logos, colors, advertising, marketing, uniforms, architecture, and so on. While founders and top leaders typically have the most consistent view of these matters, it's not uncommon for us to find organizations that have not codified their brands into clear and concise words. This lax discipline works okay when companies are small and tight. But as companies expand, mature, and allow more people to make decisions regarding the brand's promise and expression, this lack of codification leads to brand confusion, dilution, and misinterpretation.

For this reason, we developed "The Place Brand Constitution" to codify the brand into succinct terms. This one-page tool allows all those entrusted with representing and carrying the brand (brand stewards) to consider, compare, and contrast all decisions affecting the brand against foundational beliefs that we extract from the founders and leaders (brand authors).

Having one central document helps prevent personal opinions, conflicting agendas, and misguided views of the brand from getting into the mix and being implemented. As an organizational alignment tool and yardstick, the brand constitution is very useful as newcomers and consultants begin handling and tampering with the brand's DNA.

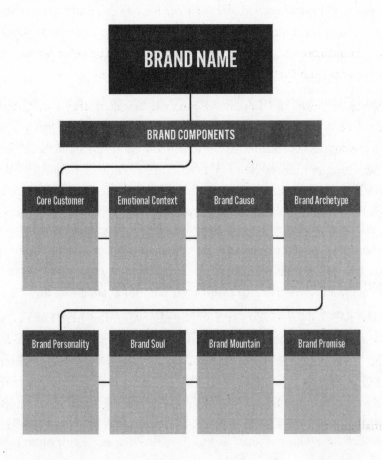

When building a brand, the more specific, precise, and consistent you can be, the stronger the brand will be internally and externally. But many companies avoid putting their brand down into succinct words because it's hard work to reach a consensus with a group of strong-minded leaders. This avoidance speaks directly to the concern and problem with everyone involved in carrying the brand having a slightly different version and interpretation of what the brand means because of a lack of codification.

One technique we use to facilitate the codification process is to think of the brand in human dimensions, not corporate terms. While getting to know a new person, you might first hear something about them (brand reputation) from a friend, colleague, or something you read. You might see a picture of them (brand image) or glimpse them from afar, which allows you to form a general impression of them.

Upon your first interaction and engagement with them, you get an immediate sense of their personality and attitude (brand personality and brand attitude) and their tone of voice. You pick up on whether they're funny, sassy, or serious. As your relationship develops over time, you learn more about their values (brand values) and how much to trust and rely on them when they "give you their word" (brand promise) to take care of something for you or others.

The most challenging quality to discover about a person is their soul (brand soul). The concept of the soul can be hard to articulate in words but relates to the more profound mystery of what the person believes in, what motivates and moves them at their core being, their integrity during good and bad times, and what gives them a particular type of aura and psychic energy. Many people and brands are hesitant to disclose this innermost part of themselves, but the more brands are willing to reveal their emotional core—by divulging the things they care about deeply—the more attractive they are to people.

For instance, think about how much we admire contestants on shows like *American Idol* for having the courage to put themselves out there in front of millions of people watching to see them sink or swim. We live vicariously through their values, spirit, and gutsiness. Brands like Patagonia and Ben & Jerry's also do this by prioritizing people or the environment over profits. Most startups I work with have "a lot of soul," at least initially. But as organizations mature, expand, and encounter challenging situations, they can lose their souls or sell them out to investors, Wall Street, or other players with different agendas.

Some have vigorously argued that companies exist solely for their shareholders' benefit and the idea of a company having a soul has no place in business. But as Marc Benioff, the cofounder, chairman, and CEO of Salesforce, said in a *New York Times* opinion piece in 2019, "It's time to say out loud what we all know to be true: Capitalism, as we know it, is dead." Citizens, customers, employees, younger generations, and even MBA students want more conscious capitalism, a term created by the maverick Whole Foods cofounder John Mackey and marketing professor Raj Sisodia. They want to see businesses serve all stakeholders—including their employees, humanity, and the environment—not just their management teams and shareholders. And most employees want to be a part of something bigger than their employer's business model or spreadsheet. They want to feel a sense of greater meaning and purpose than just making money for founders and investors.

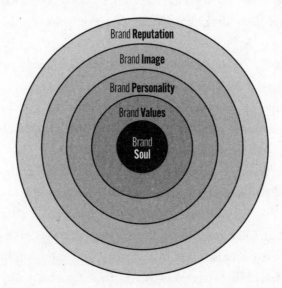

Customers also want to be part of this deeper meaning, purpose, and life force. But far too many large companies today either lack brand soul or have lost it entirely. While these giants try to layer their offerings with shiny brand images and faux "do-gooder" marketing messages, consumers have wised up to these techniques and can smell the real, genuine companies from the ones just trying to say what they think customers want to hear.

Branding today must be about real, substantive change and improvement, not lip gloss. Businesses must recognize that capitalism is changing how consumers think about society and who to buy from as well as those to avoid. The companies that succeed in the future will have to reveal their source of meaning and more about their brand soul to connect with the public.

SHARPEN YOUR SIX TIPS OF THE BRAND SPEARS

Much as the president of a nation has to remind citizens of the enduring values of their country, especially in tough times or when making difficult decisions, leaders have to regularly remind their organizations who they are, where they've been, where they're heading in the future, and which values they wish to uphold. The brand constitution does an excellent job of codifying these values and beliefs into ideals, but it's not an action plan or road map for how to get there.

To help brands reach a specific destination, we developed a customized tool called "the six tips of the brand spears." (On the next page is our interpretation of Southwest's quirky yet proprietary Brand Spears during the early days of its breakthrough success in standing out in a crowded marketplace with a unique combination lock of networked features.)

We use this resource to build consensus within the organization on what the place brand will become famous for and get clarity about which specific brand features the organization will commit to doing on a stellar level.

"Stellar" is the key word here, as most organizations take on too many initiatives, overestimate their resource capacity, and end up doing fifty things at a mediocre level. This averageness leaves their customers unimpressed and their staff dispirited, lacking the confidence and belief they can achieve great things as a team.

After decades of watching companies take on too much, we spent many years researching the appropriate number of brand initiatives an organization

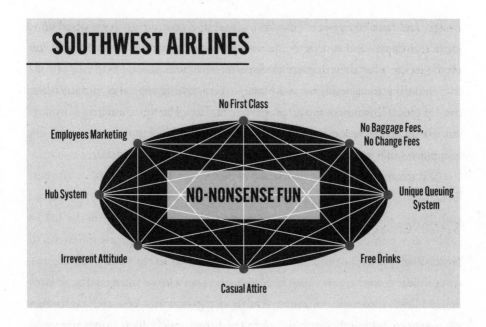

could reasonably take on and successfully achieve. Based on our experience working on hundreds of innovation projects, we discovered that, regardless of the company's size or resources, most organizations could only do about six to eight substantial brand initiatives on a stellar level. Once they got beyond that number, their ability to develop innovative ideas and execute them with precision weakened.

Despite the mythological stories of the lone genius, innovation is not always about finding a rare talent who can come up with all the breakthrough ideas and make all the winning shots. It's more about teamwork and allocating and applying human resources to narrowly-focused initiatives. The problem, however, is that most managers are spread too thin on too many goals and find themselves doing a little bit of everything. To get a better handle on this, we help our clients commit their best resources to do a handful of initiatives on a stellar level, which entails letting go of other goals and ambitions for three to five years. This commitment means they can't let others—including the top brass, board members, and family members—sneak in new initiatives on the list without an act of congress and a formal resolution to take something else off the list.

Sticking exclusively to these eight brand initiatives is much harder than it sounds, as members inside and outside your organization will lobby, warn, and plead with you to change course midstream. They will provide evidence of your competitors' actions and show you how far you're falling behind by not imitating their efforts. The temptation and pressure to add items to the menu list of "to-dos" will always be there for managers, particularly when competitors are busy chasing new goals while you're walking away from them—for the time being.

We strongly urge our clients not to add more "me-too" features to their to-do lists. If you have to change course, bring all your brand stewards together and decide which existing menu items you're willing to drop off the list to achieve this new brand initiative. Or put them in the queue of new initiatives to pursue after you've accomplished the first batch of six to eight stellar objectives.

Deciding on the narrow set of initiatives takes a lot of internal discussions, debates, and consensus-building. And sticking to a strategy and game plan takes a lot of discipline, fortitude, and the courage to let others down and withstand criticism while you stay focused on your primary objective. For example, in a delivery-obsessed world, Trader Joe's doesn't deliver, not even during the pandemic. According to a May 2023 episode of the grocery chain's podcast, *Inside Trader Joe's,* "We believe the store is our brand, that what happens within the four walls of your neighborhood Trader Joe's is a huge part of what makes Trader Joe's special." Matt Sloan, vice president of marketing at the grocer, noted that eCommerce channels, especially delivery, "would only just add cost" that would detract from the resources that the grocer can invest in that in-store experience. No matter the pleas and pressure, they demonstrate tremendous resolve and conviction in focusing their resources on creating in-store experiences that draw people to them in droves.

Similarly, Costco has focused its limited resources on excelling at a narrow set of goals, such as having under 4,000 items for sale in each warehouse store, whereas a Walmart supercenter sells 142,000 items. This limited assortment allows Costco's procurement team to rigorously screen and test each product to ensure it's the best product at the best price for its customers who have come to rely on the brand's commitment to quality curation and its elimination of the paradox of too many run-of-the-mill choices.

The secret to these mega-successful brands is having the discipline to do better with less and "just say no" to adding more things on their to-do lists. But understandably, many questions arise when working with clients on the six spear tips. Below you'll find our answers to the most common ones.

Are the Six Brand Tips Permanent?

While the Brand Constitution is more enduring, the six tips of the brand spears should change periodically. We recommend clients stick to a plan of achieving the first six tips for at least three years before advancing to the next six tips.

How Will We Know When We Have Achieved a Level of Stellar-ness?

When consumers can state with clarity what your brand is about and what it stands for, when the media gives you the top award for, say, the best slice of pizza in the city, or when your competitors acknowledge you're the market leader for this particular category.

Most consumers can list out what brands like Apple, Nike, or Lululemon do exceptionally well. While they don't always say the exact same words or use the same terms, they usually hit on the essence of the idea with remarkable consistency. Of course, these six tips of the spear need to support and roll under a larger umbrella idea or central concept of the brand, which we call the "brand acorn" because it contains the core seed and origin story of the company's mission, purpose, and cause for making the world a better place.

Are the Six Tips of the Brand Spears What We Already Do Well, or What We Want to Do Better?

How we use the brand spears can vary depending on the type of organization we're working with, the consumer context, their competitor dynamics, and specific industry limits. Some organizations, particularly older, multigenerational companies, tend to forget their values or lose sight of what made them famous in the first place, which can dilute the brand meaning. Often, due to this lack of clarity, they can even set initiatives that go against their core values. In these cases, we have a serious conversation with leaders about what legendary aspects they've lost or marginalized versus what core brand features they should resurrect and return to a level of stellar-ness.

But for those companies that already know and live their values, we use the brand spears to help them focus on what it will take to elevate the brand to the next level of excellence for the next three to five years. This commitment requires an organization to let go of maintaining things in a status quo manner and start thinking about what kind of additional resources, process changes, and bold innovation initiatives are necessary to rise to a new, idealized level. This ambitious reach is not meant to break the back of the organization but, instead, to stretch its capabilities to achieve a new level of brand excellence. However, we still have to be extra careful and realistic about what the organization can reasonably achieve in these three to five years.

How Do We Get the Organization Behind the Six Tips?

The brand spears are not only a brand management tool but also an internal brand communication tool to help focus your organizational resources on the most critical objectives. Achieving this level of concentrated effort requires top leaders to set and communicate the vision for where they want the organization to head going forward. It can't—and shouldn't—be handed down the ladder, as this arrangement will allow more senior folks to bypass and overrule the strategy. The top leaders must be committed to the goals behind the objectives and fully support the allocation of resources. If not, they'll have a lofty vision that never gets any traction or movement on the ground.

Most organizations can't just get better on their own. They usually need specialized experts, consultants, coaches, and trainers to hold them accountable for sticking to their game plan. In most cases, we work with organizations to create a series of special task forces with professionals from both inside and outside the organization that can understand the conceptual nature of each of the brand spearpoints and develop a strategy, process, and plan for how to get there. Mid-level managers are typically good at this and can thrive off having a complex but narrow goal. But again, there has to be senior-level buy-in and participation from the top, or the initiative will not make it across the finish line intact.

Admittedly, there is usually significant resistance to organizational change, but leaders can make a big difference in channeling the energy of employees in the right direction by not *telling* them they have to do this, but rather by *asking* them, "How can we achieve this particular goal?" That's when team members feel involved in the change process and get excited about coming up with new and different ideas outside of the standard procedures.

In many decades of doing groundbreaking prototypes that raise the bar and change the rules for how an industry competes, I've found achieving small successes is the most advantageous way to effect change and build momentum in an organization, as it helps foster a problem-solving organization and an innovation-based culture.

Should the Six Tips of the Brand Spears Be Interrelated?

The challenge many businesses face is creating a proprietary product that stands out in the crowd and is hard for competitors to replicate. We live in an era where knowledge, manufacturing processes, and even trade secrets are easy for competitors to find, copy, and emulate. The primary difference between one product and the next in many categories often comes down to price, availability, and the subtle differences in features, trust, and attitude, which puts increased pressure on the brand to tilt the scale.

For this reason, the six spear tips should not be a list of unrelated "me too" components, which competitors can easily follow like a standard recipe and ingredient mix. Ideally, the six spear tips should represent an interconnected network of unique and synergistic features that create a hard-to-match combination lock. The more bold, daring, and abnormal this brand network is, the more likely your competitors will not emulate your code, which is why it behooves companies to do things competitors wouldn't dare do.

Maximize

"The greatest danger occurs at the moment of victory."

—Napoleon Bonaparte

THE MAXIMIZATION PHASE HELPS OUR clients ensure they capture the full value and impact of a place once it's built and in operation. This step entails adding a series of ongoing brand maintenance tools to monitor their place's health, vitality, and livelihood, which keeps the brand on track and increases market leadership potential. In the pages that follow, we'll break down the tactics we've developed to accomplish this, including:

- Using speed as a strategy
- Bringing in "fresh horses"

- Establishing a "brand stewardship committee"
- Ingraining "brand as culture"
- Considering the "3 out of 10" clients that do groundbreaking work

USE SPEED AS A STRATEGY

In the boxing arena, there's a phrase old-time coaches frequently yell to their up-and-coming fighters: "Stop posing!" They shout this warning from the corner of the ring because after apprenticing boxers throw a solid punch, they tend to pause for a split second to admire their handiwork as if posing for a camera. This slight break in action opens the door for a more seasoned opponent to clobber them with an ambush of counterpunches.

No matter how great a boxer's one punch is, coaches demand their students "get busy" throwing a flurry of punches to ensure they don't lose their positive momentum. They expect their apprentices to use speed as a strategy of following up one good hit with another because it dulls the enthusiasm of their competitors, shakes their confidence, and makes them hesitant about entering the boxer's space.

The same strategy applies to innovating places. Swiftness and suddenness are particularly important when rolling out a new, innovative prototype concept in the retail, food, and housing industries. However, many organizations deliver one great punch to the market and then pause to admire their work or pose for the press tour for too long while their competitors (and their consultants, like our firm) study their concept inside and out.

Similarly, many retail companies will open a new, innovative prototype and then put it through the "committee process," which can lead to analysis paralysis, all while their more agile competitors quickly copy the best features of the concept and knock off key parts of the strategy. Many retailers have won top honors in their field for completing one great project punch before waiting three to five years to find the next location. This approach is like a great kid's movie franchise that takes ten years to follow up with a sequel. By that time, their fans have grown up and moved on to the next big thing in their life. Retail clients need to strike while the cultural iron is hot and not let the momentum of their one great punch fade.

Our most successful clients start proactively planning for the second, third, and fourth locations of their innovative prototype once they see the strength of the concept on the drawing boards. Admittedly, this takes guts and involves calculated risks and the potential for mistakes, but this conviction is what it takes to create a sizable advantage over your competitors and maintain your leadership position in the market. Business leaders often ask me what makes the Texas-based grocery brand H-E-B one of the most successful food and grocery retailers. While their execution is remarkable, their appetite for continually trying new ideas to raise the bar for what a grocery store can be for the consumers they serve is fearsome. Few retailers want to compete head-to-head with H-E-B because they will outmaneuver, outpunch, and outsmart anyone who steps into their ring. Most importantly, they aren't afraid to make mistakes in an industry that historically doesn't tolerate them.

While some clients only have one location and don't have plans to build more venues, this doesn't mean they should set their place up once with one big flashy punch and then rest on their laurels. Single-location places also need sprucing up, overhauling, and reenvisioning lest they get stale and outdated.

As harsh as the terms "fighting," "punching," and "dominating" may sound, the business of attracting people to your place—whether you're a retail store, museum, urban district, or university—is a competitive sport and an increasingly brutal battlefield. You don't see companies like Walmart, Amazon, or Netflix apologizing for wiping out the local bookstore on Main Street, the third-generation family-owned sporting goods store at the neighborhood shopping center, or the historic cinemas going out of business. These giants play for keeps, and so should you.

If local retail players want to hold on to their trade areas and keep their competitors at bay, they'll have to take command of their ring and capitalize on a new concept's momentary advantage. But no matter how great the innovative idea is, market advantages don't last long, particularly for local and regional retailers vulnerable to well-funded national and international competitors.

Smaller organizations must use speed, suddenness, and rapid-fire follow-up techniques to keep the invaders from raiding their territories.

BRING IN FRESH HORSES

After completing a new project, the client, consultant, and contractor teams are usually exhausted, worn out, and sleep deprived. Their ability to focus, much less "freak out" anymore about the last remaining details and finishing touches, is usually not as sharp as it was initially. For this reason, we like to bring in fresh horses and fresh eyes from our office to study the project after completion to conduct a post-evaluation phase and make comprehensive recommendations on how the project can be further improved, enhanced, and tweaked to maximize its success potential. Far too often, we see an innovative project that could've been even better if the core team wasn't so exhausted from working on it, but it's critical to success that both clients and consultants develop strategies to identify and eke out these additional gains.

Some common things we typically learn from opening a new project include post-opening items such as lighting levels, temperature adjustments, sound issues, flow problems, pinch points, and so on. But the more significant opportunities come from using the ten questions we presented in chapter seven, the "on-site observations," to study how consumers and employees behave in the space and observe where customers are most social, where they're enjoying their time, and where they're not.

We also learn volumes by studying customers in stores to see what attracts their eyes and attention, as discussed in chapter three. And most importantly, we get to think critically and strategically about what adjustments we'd make in version 2 (V.2) of the prototype.

Like automobile or software development, the prototype development process is rarely finished in one big push. To get a place brand and customer experience running at its peak performance level, it usually takes two to four iterations to maximize its success potential.

We wrap up this step with a post-evaluation workshop and review session with the client to strategize how to reach a higher level of performance in the existing venue and future versions.

APPOINT A "BRAND STEWARDSHIP" COMMITTEE

Most companies have detailed processes, procedures, and meetings focused on accounting, tax planning, legal, and human resources. But imagine if you didn't attend to your accounting books and tax situation for three to five years. They'd be an utter mess and put your company at significant risk. This negligence may sound irresponsible. Yet this is what many companies' "brand books" look like when we arrive. They haven't put the brand on the lift or given it a tune-up or alignment in over a decade and wonder why things are off course and not running well. To keep your brand in tip-top shape, we recommend the following:

1. **Appoint someone internally to serve as the Chief Brand Officer** (CBO) to be accountable for leading the brand strategy and maintenance, similar to having a Chief Financial Officer (CFO) or head of legal or HR. If your organization is small, one of the leaders can add this duty to their list of responsibilities. If possible, I encourage organizations to have their first CBO be one of the company's top executives or founders. This way, the brand will get the close parenting and nurturing it needs to grow into a strong, capable entity.

2. **Establish a brand stewardship committee** that meets regularly to monitor the brand's health, vitality, and livelihood. The individuals who make up this stewardship committee should consist of those strategic leaders involved in making decisions that affect the brand's evolution. If necessary, this group can serve terms on a rotating basis to gain broader participation.

The first task of the brand stewardship committee is to establish a master list outlining all of the company's various brand programs, efforts, and initiatives. Next, we establish a priority and hierarchy for those brand initiatives that the organization believes it can realistically achieve in a three-year time frame.

The primary duty of the brand stewardship committee is to ensure that the list of brand initiatives is reasonable to achieve, given the available resources. This group should establish a master list outlining the company's various brand programs, efforts, and initiatives. Next, it should establish a priority and hierarchy for those brand initiatives the organization believes it can realistically achieve in three years.

CEMENT BRAND AS CULTURE

Getting the first few meetings of the brand stewardship process started can be challenging, particularly if the brand is in rough shape, the innovation targets are all over the place, and the programs are cloistered in territorial departments. It helps to have an outside facilitator organize the priority of discussion topics and keep the conversation focused on brand-related issues and not drift into other operational issues. The more times this group meets to talk about the brand's health, vitality, and livelihood, the more the management team will get comfortable sharing ideas, reaching a consensus, and building a unified vision around the brand promise, values, and beliefs.

The real power of this committee is deputizing a group of leaders to become black belt evangelists and shepherds of the brand who can then train the next level of employees to uphold and maintain the values. Over time, a stronger brand narrative and set of values and beliefs take hold of an organization and become a permanent part of its culture.

But the glue that holds a culture together and makes them have a tight bond with others is not management hierarchy protocols, process decision trees, or employee reviews. It's the belief in the meaning and purpose of the brand and the community of caretakers that ensure its safety and protection.

Next to having the right vehicle (the prototype), building an army of believers in your brand starts first and foremost with the strength and commitment of the brand stewardship committee.

BE A 3 OUT OF 10

When I started working with organizations in the late 1980s, I assumed every company or institution could achieve greatness with the right insights, tools, and action plan. But as I matured, I realized not all companies are willing to make the sacrifices required to be great and instead spend their time frustrated and stuck in average positions. My staff and I used to take this averageness as a failure on our part. But after a few decades of doing this type of work, we realized that only about 3 out of 10 companies could do groundbreaking, breathtaking, and game-changing innovation work. The other seven will do better than where they started but won't reach the level of excellence they initially desired.

One thing we're good at as a firm is noticing patterns, decoding behaviors, and categorizing things into typologies. So, for over three decades, we've studied why the 3 out of 10 organizations break new ground while the other seven can't seem to get there.

We looked at the issue of size and wondered if big companies do better because of their deep pockets and resources or if small companies do better because of their narrow focus and less bureaucratic leadership protocols. But that wasn't the deciding factor. We also studied the age of companies, start-ups versus mid-career organizations versus mature companies, but that wasn't always the deciding factor. We analyzed whether it was public companies versus privately held companies. While there were some critical process issues that required a unique approach, that didn't make a critical difference either. We explored if there was something we were doing in our approach to make some companies achieve their goals versus those who didn't, but that wasn't the deciding factor. We wondered if companies that stay out of our hair and let us do what we believe is right for their brand works better than having them heavily involved in the process, but it doesn't. We need and value the pushback from clients as it helps to sharpen our axes and refine our thinking to a sharp point.

Although it took some time to break down the client typologies, what we discovered is that the "3 out 10" companies have the following characteristics:

A Devoted Brand Champion

The most innovative companies have one senior-level person in the organization who serves as the Brand Champion of our mission to carry the enterprise from the badlands into the promised lands of exploring new opportunities. This advocate doesn't block or give us everything we want. Instead, they help us navigate the organizational network and map out what it takes to get great ideas through the layers and committees. Similarly, they continually remind the organizational leaders of the purpose of the innovation journey and help remind managers why they need to let go of past ways of doing business. The Brand Champion serves as a coach, advisor, mentor, interpreter, and cheerleader when consultants or internal management teams feel down, dispirited, or discouraged by external events.

One of the best Brand Champions we've ever worked with is Tom Herman, the senior vice president of Northgate Gonzalez Market, a family-owned Mexican grocery store chain in Southern California. When Tom sees a great strategic vision, even if it's bold and risky, he's dogged about developing it further and won't let go until he gets it across the finish line.

In every "3 out of 10" job we've ever done, there was a strong Brand Champion at the table, and in every "7 out of 10" project with less than stellar results, there wasn't a Brand Champion there to help escort, defend, and ensure the innovation process succeeds.

An Open Mind About Potential Outcomes

"If you don't know where you're going, any road will take you there." There's a lot of truth in the oft-cited but not entirely accurate quote from Lewis Carroll's classic children's tale *Alice's Adventures in Wonderland*. Despite the discomfort unpredictability causes some managers, when companies embark on an innovation journey, there is no step-by-step road map and guaranteed way to get there, only vague hunches about which direction to head in. If a clear path were visible, it wouldn't be that innovative.

The beautiful thing about the innovation process is you're never entirely sure where you are in the journey or what you might find along the way. For the "3 out of 10" companies, the potential discoveries and rewards are worth the uncertainty and risk. But some organizations require knowing exactly where they're going and what they will uncover ahead of time. Because of the low risk, this predictable path will yield average rewards and generate brief advantages that any competitor can achieve with a little research.

The CEO of the Southern California grocery store chain Gelson's, John Bagan, is another Brand Champion we greatly admire because he consistently encourages and inspires our team to think big and push the boundaries of what a grocery store can be and mean to its customers. He's not afraid of breaking the industry rules or exploring different ways of "going to market." If anything, he expects us to challenge conventional wisdom and venture beyond the standard best practices.

A Consistent Group of Participants from Beginning to End

Great companies put two continuous equations together well. The first equation has the right talent, discipline, and conviction to innovate. The second factor surrounds that first equation with the right strategy, timing, and luck. But where companies get themselves in the ditch is a lack of conviction and consistency.

The innovation process entails a certain amount of career risk and making big, bold bets on the future on behalf of an organization. As consultants, we're there to investigate and minimize these risks. But true innovation ultimately requires clients to take that leap-of-faith bet on the future eventually. The "3 out of 10" companies that do game-changing work have a consistent and tight-knit integration of leaders and consultants that make that bet together as a united, convicted team. But when that group has new managers and consultants enter the process midstream, it can split the team dynamic and dilute the conviction. These new entrants feel compelled to play the devil's advocate to demonstrate their worth in front of their new peers or desire to change the direction of the journey to leave a public fingerprint of their own on the efforts.

The "7 out of 10" companies with mediocre gains frequently have a changing of the guard somewhere in the middle of the process that disrupts the dynamic flow and conviction of the team. But "3 out of 10" companies commit to the journey from beginning to end with the same core team and conviction.

Stick-to-it-ness

It's not uncommon for us to turn down new projects with potential clients because we don't believe they have the stamina and conviction to stick out the uncertainty of the innovation process to the end. While they might claim they want to achieve big breakthroughs, a highly bureaucratic organization without a Brand Champion or determined leader will often give up too quickly on a new idea because of the internal political risks, the lack of immediate sales gains, or the patience required to get through the inelegant parts of the mission.

I find that most organizations stuck in the good-but-not-great position give up too quickly on innovation efforts, particularly if their first iteration doesn't instantaneously catch on with the board or produce immediate results versus troubleshooting, workshopping, and adapting. This mindset is common in organizations heavily focused on operations and efficiency. But nurturing a culture of innovation and experimentation is critical to keeping an organization at the forefront of its industry versus always trailing behind the times. To become a "3 out of 10" innovator, organizations must have the patience to recognize the value of an insight, the determination to keep tweaking it, and the stick-to-it-ness to not give up midway but see it through to the end. Of course, not every new idea or concept will make it. You must, however, keep pitching and launching new ideas with enough leadership force to break through the atmosphere of doubt and conventionalism.

An Ability to Execute

Although my team and I might spend thousands of hours planning, designing, and building a new race car for our clients to win their industry race, they must ultimately be the ones to drive it across the finish line. But if they don't know how to drive a faster car, can't handle the pressure of a high-performance vehicle, or cope with the twists and turns involved in a heated innovation race with aggressive competitors, their new concept can end up in the ditch.

For this reason, we spend a lot of time with our clients, assessing their abilities to drive new ideas through their organization and execute a more advanced prototype concept on high-speed racetracks, but sometimes we overestimate what they can do. For instance, we once developed a new prototype concept for a retailer that focused on the deep symbolic meaning and psychological value that tables—whether the dining room table, breakfast table, or backyard patio table—represent in the home. We designed a series of beautifully merchandised table vignettes / solution zones throughout strategic locations in the store, outfitted with carefully curated products for sale that offered seductive lifestyle solutions that could help customers bring their table to life for the holidays, seasons, and everyday occasions. The client only needed to source the items and set the tables up seductively from a merchandising playbook, but even that simple task turned into a massive struggle. Much to our shock, we discovered our retail client was secretly ordering items from Amazon because they couldn't figure out how to source them on their own. This realization spoke to a much bigger problem they had within their organization's capabilities to drive new concepts and execute new ideas: it begged the question if they deserved the increased patronage they sought from customers.

The big question organizations need to decide up front is whether they want to pursue incremental tweaks to their brand experience that are copyable, nonproprietary, and short-lived. Or do they have the confidence to swing for the fences and make game-changing innovation moves that will take years, if not decades, for others to figure out, much less catch up to?

This statement is not a dare but a realistic assessment of whether it's best to stay on the old shore of your industry and make slight adjustments to your beachhead or venture out on the high seas to discover new lands and break new ground. Trying to hit a little bit of both is not advisable. It confuses staff and throws off the conviction and commitment of the team.

PLACE BRANDING IS NEVER DONE

A senior manager once walked into the middle of a strategic brainstorming session at a corporate headquarters to announce to his peers that he couldn't wait until this "branding stuff was done" so that they could "get back to focusing on operations," even while the business was rapidly losing market share and connection to its core customers. Unfortunately, focusing on operations alone doesn't create sufficient demand.

As much as some would like the branding process to be a one-and-done exercise, like accounting, legal, and product development, the branding process is never finished. Instead, it requires constant upkeep, evaluation, and vigilance to maintain and manage, lest it fall out of order.

Business experts frequently talk about "building a brand" as if its representation is a permanent structure. But this thinking isn't as stable or durable as it sounds. Once a brand becomes static and affixed to an era or generation, it can lose touch with the changing culture of the times while its core audiences age out and younger generations seek to differentiate themselves. Iconic brands like Cadillac, Jell-O, Tide, Gap, Victoria's Secret, Applebee's, Ann Taylor, Abercrombie & Fitch, and Tiffany's have suffered this worrisome fate to varying degrees. Some pulled out of their slump by introducing radically different formats, while others couldn't regain their cultural groove.

Speaking of groovy and showing my age, I prefer to think of a brand as a fluid, evolving entity, much like music. A musician or band must first uncover its distinctive voice and then have something relevant to say about its times to attract an audience. But to stay relevant over the decades, these artists must keep pushing the boundaries of where music, fashion, and culture are heading. If not, they risk becoming an oldies but goodies band, playing the same tired songs at birthdays, bar mitzvahs, and high school reunions.

To keep places relevant and top of mind, the bonfire master—a.k.a. customer experience officer, DJ, and master of ceremonies—should play some of their customers' favorite but predictable tunes while simultaneously turning them on to the hottest new acts and sounds that reflect the aspirations of their culture and aren't laughably behind the times. While keeping up with the fashion of the times requires a committed team of culture-seekers, trend-watchers, and cool-hunters, this work is essential for brands to stay relevant.

PART FOUR

Making Everyday Places Extraordinary

"Architecture is largely a discipline that sits on stilts, away from the floodlands of the people that use it in everyday life."

—Amy Schellenbaum

I WOULDN'T BLAME ANYONE FOR assuming my passion is the business of retail and the science of selling, particularly with the volume of strategies presented in this book for attracting customers, increasing sales, and shaping consumer behavior. But I'm not a Capitalist at heart; I'm a dyed-in-the-wool Creator who loves bringing people together around magical bonfire moments that foster deeper social connections and interactions, which, I believe, happens at the intersection of commerce and community. It took me a while, however, to come to this viewpoint.

When I started working in the design profession in the late 1980s, the transition from the idealism of architecture school—where there were no profit-driven clients, P&L statements, or stock price issues to contend with—to the reality of working with real-world clients was abrupt, if not depressing, for a creative thinker. After several years of trying to reconcile these two worlds, I experienced a simultaneous career crisis and awakening. Through my efforts to represent my clients' best interests, I saw how things worked in boardrooms, Wall Street, Main Street, and city council meetings. I witnessed the challenges my clients faced in putting together the financial backing for capital-intensive projects and the battles they lost over revenue projections, operating costs, and the regulatory review process. But more than anything, I noticed how deeply ingrained the laws of economics, business, and capitalism infiltrated every layer of society, including architecture, and I learned firsthand how business concepts shaped our lives, laws, politics, and culture, whether we liked it or not.

Whenever I listened to Presidents of the United States address our nation, they always talked about the economy, GDP, interest rates, unemployment rates, and the number of jobs created. They'd save some room to discuss equal rights, education, medical advancements, the space race, and social justice. But rarely, if ever, did I hear them reference the importance of how architecture shaped our country's health, vitality, and civility. I believed architecture played a key role in shaping our world and wanted it to be relevant to leaders. But instead of trying to bend the universe toward seeing the world through designers' eyes, I realized that architects needed to do a better job of relating their value and contribution to the economy and the business world. This insight led my colleagues and me to explore a new approach to architecture that would integrate business, science, and design into a system of thinking.

When I tried to enlist the architectural academy into this exploration, the mere suggestion of blending these seemingly disparate fields rubbed their academic hairs and artistic beliefs the wrong way. One of my professors went as far as to declare that "retail is the single most corrosive force on design and the enemy of architecture." I thought long and hard about his use of the word "force" and decided to study commerce and capitalism as a force on architecture, just as I had studied the forces of wind, earthquakes, and termites. While I'm not a big fan of termites, learning about how they work as a force of nature and an army of destruction on building materials greatly informed my architectural design process. Likewise, studying the concepts of retail, capitalism, and economics helped me see architecture in a different light and connect better to the issues and concerns businesses and institutions faced. These epiphanies inspired my team and me to develop a new approach to design that was more relevant to average consumers and local businesses. However, it was easy to see the inequality of who receives the best design thinking and those who rarely get access to it, so I made it my personal mission to correct this imbalance where I could.

I don't worry about the wealthy or cultural elite accessing the best talent in the design profession—as they often run in the same circles. I worry about the overlooked communities, the forgotten people, and the small, hardworking entrepreneurs who hardly ever benefit from the best designers.

If I were Bill Gates or MacKenzie Scott (Jeff Bezos's ex-wife), I could donate a billion dollars to help the forgotten, overlooked, and hardworking trying to make ends meet, but all I have to offer are my design talents, cultural insights, and strategic advice. And the best way I know how to use those skills is by helping these overlooked audiences create environments that harness the power to convene people in place, attract the public to their places of business, and enhance their sense of community and belonging.

As a proud parent of hundreds of projects, each one is a permanent part of me and forever etched into my soul. While I've had the privilege of working with some of the world's leading brands and institutions, two unassuming projects hold a special place in my heart because they remind me why I got into architecture in the first place, which was not to make beautiful objects but to make the general public feel beautiful in places. They are my "tombstone projects" because they helped those who never had access to good design but needed it the most.

In the final two chapters of this book, I unfold how my colleagues and I used our time, talents, and training to make these everyday places better for the people and communities they serve. The first project involved transforming a formerly blighted urban district into a bustling "work, live, and play" district in my old stomping grounds of Charlotte, North Carolina, which gave me a life lesson in the power of vision and community. The second project entailed turning an ordinary all-you-can-eat steak buffet restaurant chain that catered to customers with limited means and fixed incomes into the most meaningful moment of their week, which helped me see the transformative power of making everyday places extraordinary.

Plenty of talented architects can design a multimillion-dollar museum or skyscraper. The harder, less sexy challenge is finding designers willing to use their training to turn around a blighted urban district with an annual working budget of $20,000 or use their sophisticated design talents to make a smorgasbord of mashed potatoes, carrots, and meatloaf become the highlight of some forgotten soul's week.

CHAP TER ELEVEN

The Little Engine That Could

"Never doubt that a small group of thoughtful, committed citizens can change the world. Indeed, it is the only thing that ever has."

—Margaret Mead

"I'M PRETTY GOOD WITH MATH," the chairman of the nation's largest bank said facetiously, "but I can't figure out how you're getting more done with an annual operating budget of $20,000 than we are with the millions we collect downtown each year as part of our district taxes. So I gotta ask: What's the secret?"

"With all due respect, sir," I began carefully, "the uptown leaders sell prestige to the big shots who already have loads of status. But our district sells the opportunity for ordinary folks to be a part of making history. The mistake I see many downtown districts make is thinking what will bond supporters to them is how polished, shiny, and finished their place is, but I believe it's the opposite. Humans have a deep, psychological need to fix up their environment and repair broken things. They want to leave their handprints on a place that needs saving and attention, so we give them an easy way to do that here. That's the first half of our secret sauce."

"What's the other half?" he asked before I could lay it on him.

"We've got Tony!"

Everyone in Charlotte knew Tony Pressley. He was the self-made developer who invested in run-down areas most people overlooked, which is precisely where my business partner, Terry Shook, and I found him.

It was the early 1990s, and Terry and I were just getting our new strategic design firm off the ground. We needed to find a bigger office space but couldn't afford the sky-high rents downtown, never mind the monthly parking fees. We knew going to the suburbs to sit in a drop-ceiling office cubicle maze would suck every ounce of creativity out of us. So, like Tony, we looked around at the places everyone else dismissed and found a few diamonds in the rough in a part of the city called the South Boulevard Corridor. I never liked the word "corridor." It sounds like an area you pass through, not a place you want to live, work, or hang out in. But it was a common term in the 1980s and '90s that described the "hub and spoke" model of many cities across the U.S. where the arterial roadways radiate from the established urban core to the shiny new suburban communities.

These two extremes—the downtown and the suburbs—typically got all the attention, infrastructure, and investment dollars, while the corridors linking these areas were consistently passed over for economic development opportunities. This pattern led to high unemployment rates, low homeownership, increased crime, and the inevitable hazards of abandoned properties.

Adding insult to injury, the transportation engineers routinely viewed these corridor streets as pipes, not places with pedestrians, families, and businesses. In their relentless quest to widen lanes for more vehicular throughput, they ripped out not only sidewalks, trees, medians, and local shops but also the personality and spirit of the neighborhoods, making these areas feel harsher, more undesirable, and less safe. While I understood the need to get more people through the city, I never understood why they had to destroy historically significant parts of the community on their way out to the burbs. People blame the inhabitants of these areas for living and working in such squalor, but government planning frequently makes these "corridors" uninhabitable and undesirable for investing.

Terry and I always believed these corridors had tremendous community capitalism locked inside them. They just needed the right vision, tools, and leadership structure to repair the damage to their environment and unleash their greater potential.

When we met Tony, he was renovating an old factory complex called Atherton Mill in the South Boulevard Corridor, one of several commuter corridors in the city. While he went through incredible effort and expense to rehabilitate this historic complex into raw, open space, it was still a tough sell for many businesses to dare locate in this "no-man's-land." But for a new startup like ours, the rents were attractive, and the opportunity to help rebuild an urban corridor was exciting. We signed up for the challenge and became one of the first few charter tenants to locate in the old textile mill alongside another early pioneer, a vintage antique, art, and furniture shop called Interiors Marketplace.

Since my partners, Terry, Frank, and Stan, and I had spent many years working downtown, setting up shop in a blighted urban corridor was a change of pace. But we were motivated by the sense of purpose, meaning, and soul that came from working inside an old factory building. We were also surprised to see how much fulfillment came from rescuing other old buildings—or what Frank called "the beauty of the found object"—in the area versus designing yet another new and shiny structure. And luckily for us, the South Boulevard Corridor was chock-full of these old-soul buildings that desperately needed saving and a second chance at life.

Although many of our early advisors couldn't understand why we'd establish our new office in this run-down area, most of the South Boulevard Corridor buildings had great bones and craftsman-like character underneath their layers of grit, grime, and graffiti. They just needed some design love and a cosmetic makeover to allow their hidden beauty to shine through, which we were good at doing resourcefully on a lean budget. So once we finished setting up our own office, we got to work restoring many other properties in the area for the "risk-oblivious" tenants bold enough to locate their business in the corridor.

The area, however, still struggled to take off because of its perception as harsh, blighted, and unsafe. If we wanted to unlock the greater potential of this area, we had to change the district's image and create a desirable brand address. But we faced a series of seemingly impossible challenges. (While I'll present our solutions sequentially, they happened in more of a concurrent manner with varying fuse lengths.)

THE NEED FOR ADOPTIVE PARENTS

Urban corridors can sometimes be like orphans. Instead of getting the daily nurturing and care they need, these corridors often become wards of the state, left in the hands of overworked city planners and transportation engineers who are at the mercy of serving the most influential voices in the community (who favor spending time in the established hot spots downtown or in the suburbs and don't work, live, or know the plight of these overlooked or forgotten areas).

As an orphan area, the South Boulevard Corridor didn't get a lot of personal care or attention and desperately needed adoption by loving parents willing to invest more time in nurturing and developing the area. So when Tony proposed we set up a nonprofit organization to foster the district's future, I immediately jumped on board as one of the adoptive co-parents, alongside a few other caretakers, including Gaines Brown, who set up an exhibit design firm in the corridor way before we or anyone else thought to do so.

The first thing Tony and I did was fly to Dallas to check out a revitalized urban district we'd heard many people talk about called West End. We loved the energy and vibe of this historic district and the lively tenants they attracted to their area. We filled a suitcase full of notes, sketches, and photographs during our brief stay there. Over tacos and beers, we brainstormed ways to transform the South Boulevard Corridor into a West End–like destination, which seemed like a laughable pipe dream to everyone else. Our first order of business was to get rid of the "corridor" term, image, and the view of the area as a place you pass through in favor of encouraging people to stay in and hang out. This meant taking back our streets and sidewalks, slowing traffic down, and creating a more aspirational place brand identity.

THE NEED FOR A NEW NAME AND PLACE BRAND IDENTITY

In the hotel lobby that night in Dallas, Tony and I hashed out a plan to change the name of our area from the South Boulevard Corridor to South Ind. The "Ind" referred to the formerly thriving hub of manufacturing activity during the late 1800s and early 1900s. But by the time our flight landed in Charlotte, we chickened out and settled on the more conservative and derivative name South End (which, I'll freely admit, had no historical connection or lineage to anything other than our inspirational tour of West End, Dallas).

The next day, our graphic design team went to work on exploring a series of logo and brand identity directions, including several modern, cool, and futuristic-looking logos. But the one we all gravitated to the most took what many considered the primary eyesore in the community—the old industrial smokestacks—and worked it into a central design feature of the logo, with smoke billowing out over the letters.

Some found the smokestack unflattering, but as a general rule, I've always believed in not avoiding the negative perception of a place but leaning directly into it to beat everyone's criticism to the punch and turn what some consider a negative into an advantage. Using the icon of the smokestack allowed us to develop a psychological narrative around industriousness, restoration, and resurrection, which many people in the area wanted for their community and themselves.

We used this psychological and spiritual narrative of "restoration" as a crucial part of the brand constitution we developed for South End. This decision helped turn other negative aspects into positive associations, such as "industrial strength living" for our brand attitude to explain our harsh environment, oil-stained concrete floors, and squeaky, leaky roofs to potential tenants and new residents. While we had no money, riches, or luxurious amenities to offer, our brand promise to the public was simple but profound: If they got involved and invested in this seemingly impossible quest to transform a run-down part of our city, they could become a part of "history in the making." You'd be surprised by how many people wanted to get behind that cause and join us on this seemingly impossible journey.

Even though we had no official authority to change the name of our corridor, once we settled on the South End smokestack direction, we filed our paperwork to become a 501(c)(3) nonprofit organization known as South End Development Corp.—South End for short. We then put that name-brand logo on T-shirts, hats, banners, coffee mugs, and signs. Although it took some time for it to stick, I remember the first day a TV reporter called the district by our new name on air. Despite this victory, the old South Boulevard Corridor name held strong in the halls of government, and we still had our work cut out to win that battle of naming rights.

With the brand name implanted in the ground, Tony and I went out looking for the right board members in the community to join our ambitious cause. Tony served as the first president and I as the vice president, and then later, I assumed the role of president of this nonprofit district, with Tony serving as an advisor and Dutch uncle.

THE NEED FOR A BRAND BEACON AND IDENTIFIABLE LANDMARK

The South End district was over a mile long. It lacked a cohesive fabric and a community center, or what we call the "there-there" place. Through a tremendous amount of negotiations, concessions, and plain old selling, Tony, Terry, and I were able to talk one of our new clients into locating their new restaurant concept in an old warehouse building in the district and miraculously naming their place Southend Brewery and Smokehouse. (Notice the lack of a space between "South" and "End." They insisted on that proprietary difference for their business!)

Although many of their advisors thought building a new restaurant venture in a run-down area was an unwise investment, Southend Brewery and Smokehouse became a whopping success. This award-winning hot spot, designed mostly by my partners Frank Quattrocchi and Tom Goodwin, got a lot of national attention and media buzz that helped bring a whole new crowd of visitors into the area to experience a "safe adventure" in a rough-and-tumble part of town. More importantly, the restaurant served as a symbolic beacon for our community that literally put South End on the map of every tour guide for what to see and do in Charlotte. It also provided our community with a highly visible landmark that people in the city referenced regarding location. Had we not gotten them to name their new restaurant Southend Brewery and Smokehouse, we wouldn't have captured the catalytic energy needed to show people our district was on the move and going places.

Soon after the brewery's success, other local businesses started adding the South End moniker to their name, which was a significant victory for our district because nobody would've named their business "South Boulevard Corridor Brewery." But as great as this public awareness was, we still didn't have a place for the community stakeholders to meet, which led to our next experimental initiative.

THE NEED FOR A GATHERING PLACE

Terry and I knew from previous community-building efforts that we needed to create a town hall of sorts where the key stakeholders in the community could come together to discuss, debate, and agree on the future direction of their district. So we talked Tony into letting us rent and rehabilitate an old narrow pipe shed at Atherton Mill into a gathering space to serve as South End's town hall. We used our own funds to renovate the building and branded it as The Powerhouse, which became a legendary meeting space in the community.

We held an ongoing series of public meetings, lectures, and workshops that leveraged Charlotte's desire to become a world-class city. We brought in the best minds, experts, and speakers on seemingly mundane but critical issues, such as parking, zoning, crime, development, retail, housing, transportation, and business improvement districts, all issues people in the community debated. These events were lively, heated, and often standing room only, which proved to us how much the revitalization of a district mattered to residents, local businesses, and political leaders.

In addition to the monthly lecture series, we used this space regularly to conduct envisioning workshops with residents and community stakeholders. We filled the warehouse walls with life-size drawings showcasing our district's future potential, and people from all over the city and region came to see the bold and audacious ideas we proposed for our district's future.

THE NEED FOR A PERMANENT FUNDING MECHANISM

As determined as our new board was to fix up the South End district, we didn't have the funds to do much work. To compensate, we held a never-ending series of parties, auctions, and "bake-sale-esque" events in these old warehouses to generate income. We also made many appeals for donations from the major corporations in our community, such as Bank of America, the *Charlotte Observer*, and others, who were gracious enough to help us out. Those donations, however, could only take us so far. While the events, auctions, and sponsorships provided our organization with an annual operating budget hovering around $20,000, they were incredibly time-consuming and taxing on board members. We desperately needed to find a more permanent and reliable funding mechanism for the district.

In researching how other successful urban districts solved their funding problems, we learned about Business Improvement Districts (BIDs), which in the 1990s were more common in the big northeastern cities, like New York City's Union Square, but not in North Carolina. If we wanted to create a BID for South End, however, we'd have to change state laws, which didn't allow BIDs outside of the strict downtown environments. Tony, me, and a few others on our volunteer board found ourselves lobbying politicians and setting up meetings three hours away in the state's capital, Raleigh, to change the laws.

This effort proved a time-consuming legal maze, but eventually, we got the state laws changed to allow us the legal ability to create a BID district in South End. However, we still had to get a majority of property owners in the area— most of which were absentee landowners and family trusts located outside the community—to agree to establish a self-imposed tax assessment district.

Asking property owners to tax themselves more was not an easy sell. But for the next eighteen months, I went door-to-door with an easel of drawings and charts, making our case to landowners that for a slight property tax increase, we could clean up the neighborhood, give it a better identity, and substantially enhance their property values. Some people bought it and supported us; some didn't and fought us aggressively. An urban maverick and community champion named Rob Walsh proved invaluable in this evangelization effort. At the time, Rob was the president of the downtown BID called Charlotte Center City Partners. But before that stint, he was instrumental in revitalizing one of New York's great neighborhoods as executive director of the Union Square Partnership. As a mastermind of bringing together government, academics, businesses, and local communities, Rob helped us build our coalition immensely. Although it was a struggle right down to the finish line, we eventually got the South End BID approved by the property owners and city council, which catapulted the trajectory of our district.

With a more permanent funding mechanism in place, we focused on shifting the district's image from apathetic to optimistic. We cleaned up the trash, planted greenery, and installed gateway signage, historical markers, seasonal banners, and distinctive lampposts. We held public events to build community connection and pride while hiring a full-time BID director to help us manage the increasing duties of running a growing urban district.

THE NEED FOR A PRO-BUSINESS ENVIRONMENT

Unlike Tony, most developers had no interest in touching the derelict properties in our corridor because the layers of local, state, and federal policies made investing in them nearly impossible to develop from a financial, zoning, code, and environmental liability perspective. As a result, the old historic buildings and warehouses sat empty for decades, stuck in a regulatory trap and attracting more dangerous behaviors than their policies intended to prevent.

As the old saying goes, "Capital goes where it's invited and stays where it's welcomed," but it shies away from communities and regulatory mazes that make it too difficult to invest in. In an effort to attract business dollars into our community, we had to create a pro-business environment. We lobbied politicians and worked with the city and state to develop special zoning and code provisions more appropriate to our district's historical nature and condition. We also worked with the state and other regulatory agencies on "brownfield initiatives," which involved underutilized properties where reuse was hindered by the actual, suspected, or perceived presence of pollution and environmental contaminants. Lastly, we helped identify potential businesses and tenants we thought could add great value to the area and made a concerted effort as a leadership team to pitch them our best reasons for why they needed to be in South End. Once they signed up, we ensured they got the attention and assistance they needed to navigate the local process of opening, operating, and promoting a business in South End.

These efforts made a big difference in attracting and seeding our first batch of tenants to the area. However, we still had one negative issue hurting our ability to entice investment dollars into the area: the persistent perception of crime, blight, and other undesirable behaviors.

THE NEED FOR A GEOGRAPHIC FEATURE THAT UNITES, NOT DIVIDES

While frequently overlooked, physical and geographic components within a city divide us involuntarily into groups. Fences, walls, rivers, bridges, beltways, tunnels, and mountains create a physical separation, an arbitrary "us versus them" mentality, and barriers to connecting to the "other side."

We often hear derogatory references to the "bridge and tunnel crowd" to describe people who live in communities surrounding the island of Manhattan in New York City and commute to it for work or entertainment. Or in L.A., they'll talk about those who live "in the Valley," which was reinforced worldwide in the 1983 American teen romantic comedy *Valley Girl* and suggests a "materialistic" and "airheaded" person. Every community has these pejorative, classist, and dismissive terms—shaped by physical features that make them tangible and visual—which speaks to how much we define ourselves by geographic boundaries.

While the "corridor" term in South End referenced a roadway called South Boulevard, there was also an old rail corridor that divided a lower-income neighborhood on the west side of the tracks from a more upwardly moving progressive neighborhood to the east side. The neighborhoods got along well, but the rail corridor served as a physical impediment and a symbolic hindrance to social connection.

You could track property values, homeownership, and investment dollars along this cultural divide, with one side doing much better than the other. But not only did the unsightly tracks serve as a geographic dividing line; they also served as an unmonitored zone for undesirable behaviors like drugs, prostitution, vagrancies, and crime to take place.

No matter the potential business tenants we brought through the district, the tracks were always a concerning factor and eyesore for them, not a place in their minds where people wanted to live, work, play, or build near. This view was ironic because, during the late 1800s and early 1900s, the tracks were the prime place to be. They served as a primary pipeline for transporting manufacturing goods and resources up North and down South. All the historic buildings aimed their loading dock butts toward the tracks, but there was nobody there anymore to animate the tracks other than drug dealers and drifters, and we knew we needed to come up with a solution to the problem.

To address this situation, we started by working closely with the police. We gave them space in our firm's offices and invited them to attend our monthly board meetings and give regular status reports. But after a while we realized there was only so much policing they could do to monitor the situation twenty-four hours a day. We knew there had to be a better way to turn this dividing line into a uniting line that stitched our neighborhoods together in more prosocial ways. But we knew the zipper of our community couldn't be these seedy, weedy tracks, and that's when using humor and finding the funny came into play.

During one of our brainstorming meetings, we felt severely limited by what we could do with the rail corridor and joked about putting a river down the middle of it, or an eighteen-hole golf course. "That'll attract the investment dollars," we thought. And that's when the joke hitched itself to an allied organization called the Charlotte Trolley, which also had a similar, seemingly impossible idea.

THE NEED FOR A BOLD VISION FOR THE FUTURE

After spending years meeting, planning, designing, negotiating, partnering, and lobbying the influential leaders of our community, we dared to ask the city for around twenty million dollars to run a trolley system two miles down the tracks from South End through downtown. In exchange for this seed money, we promised to return a much greater economic tax base for new real estate development activity and increased job opportunities for the city's residents, particularly those living within walking distance of the district.

Of course, the critics attacked us mercilessly, calling our trolley plan the "Folly Plan." These critics falsely assumed we were trying to develop a transportation solution when our primary goal was to create an *economic development engine* with a tangible geographic feature using the iconic, symbolic, and nostalgic trolley to get us there. We knew people wouldn't pay to overlook an unsightly railroad corridor (or a bus corridor, as the transportation engineers initially proposed and advocated) with undesirable behaviors. They would, however, be willing to pay premiums to overlook a charming, historic trolley line with sidewalks, streetlamps, bike trails, and walking and jogging paths.

Whereas most design firms would typically do a thick binder report and lengthy analysis to make their case in technical terms, Terry and I bypassed the city process and politicians' approval and created a series of what we jokingly called our "civil disobedience workshops." These meetings led us to create a simple but enticing poster with our economic development strategy and vision plan on the front and back. We then paper-bombed the community with these collectible posters. Once the developers saw the vision, they took off ahead of us and locked up all the potential sites we identified in our reports on mere speculation that something *might* happen at the fictitious trolley stations we proposed and cleverly named. Ordinary citizens and the media regularly asked the politicians when they'd get that trolley up and running in South End. Of course, the politicians jumped over each other to claim credit for the vision, which was what we wanted to happen. Our imaginary vision created an artificial demand for the properties in South End that previously everyone overlooked, ignored, or didn't want to touch, much less develop.

AN OVERWHELMING SUCCESS FROM THE "LITTLE ENGINE THAT COULD"

Today, South End is an overwhelming success story. Not only did the combined South End vision and the Trolley vision spark hundreds of millions of dollars of economic investment, but the tracks eventually became the location of the first light-rail line in Charlotte. As of March 2022, the district boasted over 4.5 million square feet of office space, 11,323 residents, 1.9 million square feet of retail and restaurants, 123 hotel rooms (and 380 more planned), 23 fitness studios, 30 salons and spas, 12 ice cream and dessert shops, and 103 locally-owned shops and restaurants. However, the biggest challenge for the district now is managing its explosive growth. This concern is where bonfire masters are so crucial for tending to the brand fire to ensure the flames of a place don't die down or grow so large that they chase people away, particularly the local businesses and residents.

Tony and I have since moved on from Charlotte. But none of this development would've ever happened had he not dared to imagine a different future for a district that others dismissed as unsightly and unworthy of investment. Although we wholeheartedly believed in the potential of South End, Terry, Tony, me, and the rest of our founding board members would've never imagined just how far this "little engine that could" story would travel or where it would ultimately take the district.

Architecture as a Social Act

"The meaning of life is to give life meaning."
—Viktor Frankl

"The question is, at what point does architecture's potential to improve human life become lost because of its inability to connect with actual humans?"
—Martin C. Pedersen and Steven Bingler

"IF YOU CAN'T TOUCH IT, it ain't real!" Percy said, pointing to the sign that proclaimed "Homestyle Cooking." As inelegant as his remark sounded, I couldn't have agreed more. Channeling the look of the Marlboro Man, Percy spent thirty-five years working at a textile mill and was skeptical of the "pointy-headed marketing suits," as he liked to call them. "They write these Hallmark card poems and expect us to believe they're real. Show me the home-cooked part!" he said, emphasizing each word.

I met Percy in the mid-1990s while he was eating his once-a-week meal at our client's 538-unit steak/buffet chain. Although I'd worked on a lot of fashionable, award-winning restaurants in my career, the buffet business was a whole other animal in the food world. This difference was because customers didn't order items from a menu at the table in front of a waiter; instead, they paid one price at the door to "eat all you can eat" in one sitting. Although not advisable, many customers tried this feat, forcing the industry to devise enticing ways to get customers to load up on the "water and air" offerings, such as salads and soups with some rolls, rice, potatoes, and stuffing packed in the gut as "filler," before digging into the high food–cost items, like meats, poultry, and seafood.

Percy was just one of the many insightful customers we interviewed to learn as much as possible about the critical decision points in the steak/buffet industry. I use the term "steak/buffet" loosely because that's how my client and their competitors referred to the restaurant category, but the order of the wording was a bit misleading.

Forty years prior, the industry *sold* roughly 90 percent steaks and 10 percent salads, and the *free* salad bar didn't exist yet. As the industry matured, though, the number of competitors increased, and this once-booming market turned into a crowded space, forcing many players to either lower their prices or come up with new features and consumer appeals. But the natural forces of commoditization were setting in, making brand differentiation and profits harder to come by and putting increased pressure on lowering pricing and cutting costs to the bone, which was not a fun business to be in.

To overcome sagging sales, some enterprising industry players started offering salads (and an array of other sides) for just one price, which was the first step to bribing customers to buy your product. What started as a four-foot all-you-can-eat salad bar with the purchase of your paid steak grew into a forty-foot double-sided island salad bar extravaganza that included an elaborate array of soups, salads, dressings, vegetables, cheese, bread, dips, desserts, and toppings, again, all for one price. Customers didn't take long to ask for the salad without the steak, which the operators agreed to, not realizing how it would forever change the industry.

Over time, the steak side of the business went from 90 percent to 10 percent while the all-you-can-eat buffet bar grew from 10 percent to 90 percent, which changed the whole dynamic of the business model. Worse, it turned the competition into an all-out slugfest focused on who could offer the most food for the lowest price. One would think the increasingly lower prices on all-you-can-eat should've concerned customers, but for some financially strapped audiences, quantity won out over quality, which made me wonder whether the design and experience of these venues even mattered. My client, however, wanted to go after those who cared slightly more for quality and experience, or what Percy called "the upwardly moving Bubbas."

If things weren't bad enough, the real boot-kick came when the more exotic-sounding steak house chains like Lone Star, Longhorn, and the ultimate '90s game changer, Outback Steakhouse, rode into town and disrupted the steak house category. Although these chains weren't from Texas or Australia, they tipped the emotional scales of customer cravings upside down, offering steaks with a rebellious attitude and some Crocodile Dundee bloomin' onions to go with it. Their saucy attitude, personality, and promise of fun stole the show. The traditional steak/buffet players found themselves out of the steak business and in a game of chicken and all-you-can-eat salad bars competing solely on price and quantity. Not long after, the top chain hired our firm to help them change the rules of their industry. But before we could come up with the creative solutions, I still had much more to learn from Percy about what problem we were really trying to solve.

"One more Big Mac and the doc says it'll come with a heart attack," he said one icy night over steaming vegetable soup, "so I try to eat as healthy as my skinny budget allows. The fixins' on this buffet are about as good as it gets for people my age trying to live off a fixed income. But this place doesn't look like where a home-cooked meal would come from, as they claim. It looks like a beat-up high school cafeteria." I felt for Percy's financial plight and others like him trying to make ends meet while avoiding fast food and eating healthier meals. My team and I saw the importance of making his date nights with the buffet special and memorable. However, there were times when I wondered what I was doing there, studying the adjacencies of the meatloaf and mashed potato trays. I couldn't imagine Frank Lloyd Wright or Frank Gehry trying to figure out where to put the macaroni and cheese on the hot bar. But something inside me told me this work makes a meaningful difference in people's lives, even if it won't appear on the cover of *Architectural Digest*.

Over a few extended meals, Percy taught me more about environmental psychology and spatial perception than any of my design professors ever did. "When restaurants talk about things like quality, service, homemade, home-cooked, or natural food," Percy said, "that's all it is—talk! The billboards, banners, TV ads, and radio spots are all smoke and mirrors. If I can't see or touch these fancy ideas like 'homemade' or 'family-style,' then it ain't real. But all I see around most restaurants is marketing sizzle, but not steak."

What I liked about Percy and many of the customers that regularly ate at buffets is they didn't mince words and always shot it to us straight. Rich people are easy to brand and charge premiums to, but those on a tight budget don't fall for clever marketing slogans or snazzy design treatments. They scrutinize their purchases and demand to see evidence and a real identifiable brand difference before forking over their hard-earned cash.

Percy's words of wisdom were consistent with my belief that no idea exists in our head without first coming through our senses. From birth, we learn to think, speak, and communicate complex ideas through sensory-rich words and metaphors that allow us to visualize people, things, or situations in simple terms. As adults, we pepper our language with tactile descriptions of people as "hardheaded," "tough as nails," "rough around the edges," "slick," "slimy," or "prickly." These sensory-based descriptions communicate vital information to others in short, succinct terms you can feel.

Over the next eight months, I'd check in regularly with Percy to share a meal and let him know how things were progressing on the new prototype design concept for the steak buffet chain. His insights and handprints were all over the final concept, which in our first batch of five beta stores more than doubled the expected weekly sales from $38,000–$42,000 to $89,000–$92,000 without changing the product, price, or service levels. The only things we changed were the context, cues, and triggers for how they presented their offerings to ensure Percy and others could touch the quality and feel the extra love and care the chain genuinely put into its products. We took the standard salad bar and turned it into the brand realm of a roadside produce stand that sells fruits and vegetables straight from the fields, communicating a freshness everyone recognizes. We brought the staff out of the back kitchen to cut the heads of lettuce, carrots, and cantaloupe right in front of the customers. Having an audience to perform in front of boosted their confidence. It made them want to be more presentable to the public, and they took more pride in the important job of preparing meals for others. We took the hot food bar, which included traditional meats, mashed potatoes, and blueberry cobbler, and turned it into the robust and meaningful brand realm of a real home kitchen. And we took the various bread, cookie, pie, and dessert products the chain offered and placed them into the brand realm of a classic bakery shop replete with a baker's hat and white apron staff, nostalgic sacks of flour, and a distinctive bell that rang every time fresh bread came out of the prominently displayed ovens.

Once we completed the new prototype stores, instead of eating dinner all by his lonesome self, Percy felt inspired to invite me to join his family and friends out for a big supper night and an evening of merrymaking at the steak/buffet chain. Even his teenage grandkids loved the new digs. Eating dinner on a fixed income was no longer an apathetic experience for low-income folks but something Percy could be proud to show off to others. Percy thanked my team and me for making his life over simple buffet meals more fulfilling, as did countless other customers.

The most illuminating compliment we got, however, was from the chain's CEO. We assumed he'd be overjoyed about doubling the weekly revenue when we met him after the grand opening to conduct our post-occupancy review and analysis. Instead, he told us to be quiet for a minute and listen, which we did, but we didn't hear anything except customers conversing over meals. "That's precisely my point!" he said. "Our customers treat us better than they ever did before. They don't carve their names on the tables and walls. They pick up after themselves, and keep the place clean. And I credit that result to something you said on the first day we met you—'environment affects behavior.' Our customers take better care of the place because it no longer looks like a prison mess hall but a respectable, aspirational place to celebrate food and family, providing our staff tremendous pride as a culture and as the new market leader."

A FORK IN THE ROAD

We eventually moved on from working in the steak/buffet segment, but I stayed in touch with Percy as a friend and mentor until his passing in 2002. His plain-talk truisms inspired me to think long and hard about my potential as an architect and what I wanted to do with the rest of my career.

Sure, I had the skills and connections to "advance my career" and "elevate my stature" by working for the wealthy 1 percent and the cultural elite with discriminating tastes. Or I could continue "slumming it with the buffet crowd," as one of my high-rise design peers jabbed. Ultimately, I stuck with the Percys, Darcys, and Ernies of the world. Not only are they my people, but I realized that the greatest role I could play in society as an architect is to make the lives and experiences of everyday people better, more experiential, and, above all, more socially rewarding.

The whole cape and gown getup of calling myself an "Artiste" and designing self-referential monuments isn't for me. I'm good with being a design mechanic of everyday places that serve the needs and daily routines of 99 percent of the population. I find great meaning and purpose in helping place-based entities—whether mom-and-pop shops or legacy companies and established institutions—survive and thrive in an era of digital replacements.

I'm not worried about whether we'll continue having immaculately designed museums, ridiculously tall skyscrapers, and extravagant homes in society; there will be plenty of room for those public spectacle projects on the cover of architectural magazines. I'm also not worried about whether we'll continue building more ruthlessly cheap, logistically efficient, low-cost facilities.

We've got both of those extreme bases covered in spades.

But what I do worry about is who's going to save the everyday places for Percy to celebrate life on a fixed income, for Ernie to make friends and find an end to loneliness in midlife, and for my five-year-old daughter, Kaia, to develop her innate senses of the world and continue the age-old tradition of interacting with people face-to-face and socializing with friends, neighbors, and other cultures in the irreplaceable theater of life.

ACKNOWLEDGMENTS

THEY SAY EVERYONE HAS A book in them. That's true. But the tricky part is getting that book out of their heads and into a semi-coherent outline and book proposal, then through fifty rough drafts and two years of nitpicking rewrites only to realize how much better it'd be if you could start all over again now that you have a general idea of what you want to say.

While I had threatened to write a book about my work for decades, it wouldn't have happened had it not been for two extraordinary catalytic agents that came into my life at just the right time.

From the first day I met my wife in the baggage claim area of the LAX airport, Mandy believed I had something worth telling the world. She persistently poked, prodded, and pushed me out of bed early to put my theories, principles, and observations down on paper. Her unending support and faith in me kept me going through several moments of doubt when I was ready to throw in the towel. If you want to survive the ups and downs of this world, get yourself a Mandy. I can't imagine where I'd be without you by my side, Mandy. I'm here because of you!

I've been a passionate reader my entire life, so I figured writing a book would be a little easier. It wasn't. But then I stumbled upon the profoundly honest and moving articles by Michael Thompson and knew I'd found my writing coach. Michael didn't care whether I could write; instead, he got me talking about my passion for places, experiences, and branding, which helped me identify the golden nugget ideas buried within those stories. How he endured my

221

long-winded rants and constant detours to locate those kernels, I don't know. But it has something to do with his incredible patience, wit, and troubleshooting abilities, which made the daily writing process with him so much more fun and productive. Michael's a godsend for future writers and exactly the type of strategic coach all business leaders need in their corner.

Though Mandy and Michael helped turn this book into a reality, it never would've come into existence without the many other pivotal coaches who guided me through life and helped instill the values I hold today, most importantly around the importance of community. This appreciation begins with my parents, Cecil and Nina Kelley; my kids, David and Kaia; and my in-laws, Karl and Dali. It then extends to my work family, which includes my good friend and wise mentor, Terry Shook, and our extraordinarily talented principal partners: Frank Quattrocchi, Stan Rostas, Jennifer Kim, Sabrina Fan, and Jennifer Ochoa.

I also give much credit to the brilliant minds and generosity of people like Eugene Kohn, Hugh McColl, Philip Kotler, and Paco Underhill, who took me under their wings early in my career and steered me in the right direction.

And, of course, I can't forget the high school "Wrecking Crew"—Stormy, Charlie, Tim, and the Pittman Brothers—for introducing me to the Mudflats and shining a bright light on the path to building bonfire moments people are willing to crawl through mud to experience.

Lastly, I'd also like to thank my literary agent Michele Crim as well as Matt Holt, Katie Dickman, Lydia Choi, Jessika Rieck, Mallory Hyde, Kerri Stebbins, Brigid Pearson, and the entire team at BenBella Books for taking a chance on me and finding a place on their shelf for this book.

INDEX